Working Out Loud

For a better career and life

John Stepper

生き甲斐
Ikigai Press
New York

Cover design by Daniel Gomes.

Illustrations by Kazumi Koyama of 8works Consulting and by Jon Ralphs.

ISBN: 0692382399
ISBN 13: 9780692382394

For those who've felt
there could be more to work and life.

Table of Contents

Introduction

A Shift in Possibilities: My Own Story

"John, we have to make a change."

As soon as I got to his office, I knew something was wrong. It was January 2008, and my boss had arranged a special one-on-one meeting with me. He quickly started telling me that my area was being reorganized, and that I had to find a new role. I sat there, stunned. I could feel the blood rush to my face. He kept talking, but all I could think was *Why?* and *What will I tell my wife?* I left his office humiliated, angry, and afraid. I immediately started worrying about money.

Walking home, I realized how tenuous my position was and how little control I had. I was in my forties and had few meaningful connections that could help me. After ten years with the same firm, I didn't relish the prospects of working with a recruiter and having her ask, "Why are you leaving?" My career felt unstable and out of my control, and my confidence was at an all-time low. Eventually I wound up finding another project elsewhere in my department, one with less responsibility and less pay.

Looking for some kind of outlet as I was changing roles, I began using a low-tech blogging platform that was available inside the company and found it to be therapeutic. I wrote about things I was interested in, and with each post I felt like I was developing a useful skill. I wrote only half a dozen times that year, but one post about trying to use Gmail at work attracted over a thousand comments. I was amazed at how a simple essay on a social platform could make it possible to connect people and build a movement. Over time, I wrote more about social media and collaboration topics, and people from other areas in the firm started approaching me for my opinions.

Something clicked. I saw that by making my ideas and work visible, I was shaping my reputation and getting access to opportunities I wouldn't have known about otherwise.

Discovering a different kind of networking

In 2009, still conscious of my lack of helpful connections, I enrolled in a course called the Relationship Masters Academy. The course was taught by Keith Ferrazzi, the author of *Never Eat Alone* and *Who's Got Your Back?* The bulk of it took place over two intense weekends, and the people there all seemed to have bigger, more ambitious goals than me. One person, for example, had founded a charity to provide clean water and sanitation to the billion people who don't have it. He had already helped a few million people and was attending the course because he wanted to have a bigger impact. *Helped a few million people?* I listened to the others introduce themselves and became increasingly aware of my own lack of purpose.

During the course, we formed small peer support groups to practice what we were learning. I was in a group of successful bankers, which further intimidated me, and in our first session we were instructed to share something intimate about ourselves. Ferrazzi told us to avoid small talk and instead share something that few people knew and that would expose our vulnerability, something that would humanize us and make people care. One person talked about growing up as a poor immigrant and about his difficult relationship with his father. Another talked about his divorce. Those intimidating bankers became people I cared about and trusted.

My conversations outside of class changed too. When people asked me how I was doing, I stopped automatically saying "Great!" When I gave a more honest answer, I saw that being vulnerable made it easier for others to be vulnerable in return. Instead of small talk, I took an active interest in other people and found they had their own compelling story if I just cared enough to listen. My wife noticed the change. She said I seemed more excited about the people I was meeting and working with.

The habit of shipping and being purposeful

I was feeling more optimistic, perhaps, but my job hadn't changed much. Then I discovered Seth Godin. He's a bestselling author whose marketing books include *Purple Cow* and *All Marketers are Liars*, but he also writes about personal development and regularly shipping work that matters. His blog was like a multivitamin for my mind and spirit.

I started writing publicly at johnstepper.com and decided to publish every Saturday. Only sixteen people read my first post. After struggling weekend after weekend, I understood why so many people who start a blog wind up quitting. But Seth's daily posts would encourage me to "put a dent in the universe," and I kept trying. After writing for more than 200 weeks in a row, writing has become a habit and something I enjoy doing.

Developing this habit helped to expand my network and give me more confidence. I started to look at work as something that could have a greater purpose, and that, combined with Seth Godin's blog, compelled me to make more of a difference. I expanded my research and experiments at work and proposed something much more ambitious. After months of vetting a plan and presenting it to executives, I wound up in a new role that hadn't existed before, one focused on improving how people across the firm communicate and collaborate. We wound up building one of the biggest internal social networks in financial services, used regularly by more than 60,000 people.

Putting these elements together

By 2012 I felt more in control and more connected. There were still bad days and even bad months. But in those times, instead of relying on luck or lottery tickets to access a better career and life, I was able to do something about it. I made my work visible, invested in relationships, and focused on developing my skills. Although I'm still at the same firm I've been with for seventeen years, I have experienced a fundamental shift that has changed my perspective completely.

I wanted to help other people experience the same shift too. I wrote how-to guides and gave presentations. I held one-on-one sessions with people and even taught a three-month course. But none of this produced much change. Something was missing.

The key was changing habits. Over time, I realized that in addition to people learning a few skills, they needed help changing their habits so they could apply those skills regularly. After all, even though we know that exercise and a healthy diet are good for us, we still struggle with those things. So I studied how to change people's habits and learned that the research findings are remarkably consistent. They all include the need to take small steps, chart your progress, reward successes, and seek peer support. Experimenting with my own habits, I gradually became a vegetarian and started doing yoga regularly, and I no longer need the cholesterol drug I thought I would be taking for the rest of my life.

These ideas on changing habits developed into a new way to help people: coaching individuals over twelve weeks. We would start with a goal they cared about, identify people who could help with that goal, and then try to build relationships with those people based on generosity as Keith Ferrazzi taught me. Together, we practiced week after week, connecting with more people, offering more contributions, and deepening relationships.

It worked. People were shocked at their ability to connect with anyone, anywhere, at any level—and then deepen those relationships. They saw how their expanded network unlocked access to opportunities, giving them more control of their career and life and improving the odds of reaching their goal. Their previous attempts at networking were all tinged with a bad aftertaste. Now though, because they were authentic and focused on contribution, they were positive about what they were doing. They also replaced their prior ad hoc efforts with a simple, sustainable system they could go through week after week. Gradually they all developed a set of habits that would serve them well as they pursued other goals.

The aim of this book is to help you develop these same habits and experience your own shift in possibilities.

Working out loud

"Working out loud" is the phrase I use to describe both a mindset and a set of techniques you can put into practice. When I explain it to people, I say, "Think Dale Carnegie meets the Internet."[1] It's a human process more than a technical one. More than just making your work visible, you regularly frame what you're doing as a contribution and as a way to deepen relationships. You develop an open, generous, connected approach to work and life. Such a mindset combined with what you regularly put into practice is what helps you enjoy your every day and discover more possibilities.

In part III, you'll practice working out loud for yourself. You'll leverage principles for building meaningful relationships as well as modern abilities to share your work, get feedback,

1 For those who don't know Dale Carnegie, he's famous for helping people lead a better career and life. His most popular work is *How to Win Friends and Influence People*, published in 1936. Other titles include *How to Stop Worrying and Start Living* and *How to Enjoy Life and Your Job*.

and interact with others who share your interests. Importantly, you'll wrap all of this in a mindset of generosity. Even those of you who don't like technology or choose not to be visible will find that thinking of your goals in terms of relationships and contributions leads to more possibilities. All that's required is a set of skills and habits that anyone can learn.

A movement starts to form

Over the last year, to help more people apply the ideas in the book, I started forming peer support groups called "Working Out Loud circles." In a circle, each person practices building a network and deepening relationships toward a personal goal. (There's a full description in the appendix.)

When I first blogged about these circles, people I had never met starting asking how they could form them. So I sent out drafts of the book and created a quick guide, and the new circles proved to be a rich source of ideas and feedback. Before the book was even published, a small global movement started to form, and there are now circles in five countries. By the time you read this, there will be more people working out loud, more peer support groups, and a wide array of resources to help you on workingoutloud.com. While the book is complete, in many ways it feels more like a beginning than an end.

Using this book to take control of your own story

The book is divided into three parts that help you understand the elements of working out loud and how to develop the habit of doing it yourself.

Part I—For a Better Career and Life
Here you'll meet four people who created new possibilities for themselves, and you'll learn about ways to feel better about your own work and life.

Part II—The Five Elements of Working Out Loud
This part goes into the details of what working out loud is and why it works. The five basic elements are purposeful discovery, relationships, generosity, visible work, and a growth mindset. You'll be introduced to research underpinning each element and examples of how people apply them differently.

Part III—Your Own Guided Mastery Program
A guided mastery program is a form of coaching used to develop the Working Out Loud circles. The intent is to have you gradually apply a wider range of techniques while you get feedback along the way. More than just reading, you'll be learning by doing, and the repeated practice over time will transform your learning into a set of sustainable habits. If you bought this book eager to start working out loud right away, you might jump straight to part III, where you'll find techniques and exercises you can use toward accomplishing a specific goal. Then you can go back to parts I and II to give you more context for what you're practicing.

The stories, techniques, and exercises in *Working Out Loud* can help you in different ways at different stages in your career and life. If you're a new graduate looking for a job, it can help you explore career paths and build your network. If you're in midlife, it can help you enjoy the job you already have while showing you what else life might have to offer. At any age, it can help you achieve your goals and discover more possibilities.

Artwork by Kazumi Koyama from 8works Consulting after she attended a talk on working out loud. She subsequently joined a circle.

Part I

For a Better Career and Life

Chapter 1

Four Stories

Chance favors the connected mind.

—Steven Johnson, *Where Good Ideas Come From*

The subtitle of this book is "For a better career and life." But what is "better," exactly?

The best way to illustrate what I mean is through the stories of dozens of people throughout the book. For them, "better" is not an objective measure according to someone else's standards. It simply means improving their careers and lives in a way they care about, a way that's meaningful for them. The four people in this first chapter come from different backgrounds, and they vary in terms of education and social skills. They're at different stages of their lives and careers. But they all share an approach to work and life that gives them each a greater chance of enjoying their every day, gives them access to a wider range of opportunities, and increases their chances of finding meaning and fulfillment in what they do.

Jordi Muñoz, CEO

Jordi Muñoz was born in the coastal city of Ensenada, Mexico, about seventy-five miles south of San Diego. His English was limited, and he didn't go to college. In his late teens, still waiting for his green card, he found out he was going to become a father.

What do you think of Jordi's chances for finding fulfilling work?

Like most of us, Jordi had dreams of what he wanted to be when he grew up, and he tried to map those dreams to jobs he knew about. "I was very obsessed with airplanes since I was four years old. So I was always dreaming to be a pilot or probably an airplane mechanic."[1] As he got older, he began playing with computers and remote-controlled airplanes as a hobby. When he was nineteen, he joined an online community where hobbyists could share information and learn from each other. There, Jordi made his work visible by contributing designs he came up with. "I made an autopilot for my RC [remote-controlled] helicopter with accelerometers extracted from the NunChuck of Nintendo Wii."[2] He apologized online for his poor English, but other hobbyists cared more about his designs.

The person who started that community was Chris Anderson, a best-selling author, speaker, and former editor of *Wired* magazine. Chris had become interested in drones (autopiloted aircraft) as a hobby and then decided to start DIYdrones.com so he and other hobbyists could share what they were working on and learning. In his book *Makers*, Chris describes how he first noticed Jordi in that community based on the designs he was contributing. Over time,

Chris corresponded with him, and eventually they collaborated on several projects. When Chris later decided to start a company, he asked Jordi to cofound it, and it was only then that Chris learned about Jordi's background.

Normally it would have been ludicrous for Jordi Muñoz to apply for a job as CEO of a robotics company. He didn't have a university degree to certify what he knew, and his resume wouldn't have attracted any attention from a broker or on LinkedIn. There would simply be no way for his application to reach someone like Chris Anderson or to stand out if it did. But Jordi was able to shape his reputation based on his work, his passion for it, and the value other people saw in it. Jordi's contributions to the online community helped make him and his work visible, enabling him to gradually develop a set of relationships that unlocked opportunities.

Joyce Sullivan reinvents her career

For more than twenty years, Joyce worked in New York City managing complex, global projects for several big banks. At times it was challenging and well paid, even exciting. But as the banking industry changed, so did the work, and so did Joyce. When her firm downsized, Joyce was late in her career and faced with the daunting prospect of finding work in tough economic times.

When I met Joyce, it struck me how she was always interested in learning about the next new thing. Around 2006 one of those things was social media, and she started experimenting with that. She would search out entrepreneurs and social media experts who could help her learn. Using social media was just a hobby, but she was learning fast. To give herself the chance to practice using social media for work, she volunteered to serve as the chief digital strategist of the Financial Women's Association of New York, where she was already a member. Although it was an unpaid role, it allowed her to apply some of her learning in a business context. The role also helped her leverage an existing network to establish more meaningful connections and to present at conferences about social media. Each time she would learn more, make more connections, and further shape her reputation. Gradually Joyce was no longer a former banker interested in social media but a social media professional who happened to be a former banker.

While she was learning, she was helping. She would teach finance professionals about LinkedIn, organize her own networking events, and leverage her growing network by connecting people who could help each other. All of this learning and all of these connections opened up new possibilities. One of the highlights was Joyce appearing with Maria Bartiromo on CNBC "offering advice for baby boomers suddenly back at the drawing board."[3]

Over time, she combined her different skills and interests and started her own consulting firm, SocMediaFin, offering "social media strategy development and implementation for financial services and other highly regulated industries." She became a popular speaker at conferences and companies around the country, getting fulfillment from the daily interaction with her large, diverse, and still growing network. That activity made it possible for her to teach a class on social media at Baruch University and, most recently, to run professional services for a software company specializing in (you might have guessed) social media for financial services firms.

Joyce could have easily dismissed her early interest in social media with "I'm not good enough." After all, there were plenty of other people who were younger and had more experience. But Joyce kept trying new things, making connections, and getting better, and that led to new and more fulfilling possibilities.

Mara Tolja creates a new kind of job

Mara grew up in Croatia and New Zealand, spoke multiple languages, and found herself in what she described as "the worst job possible." She worked in a large firm configuring Lotus Notes databases. The work was both tedious and isolating. Few people seemed to know or care about what she did. Nevertheless, she didn't want to change firms or locations. She just wanted to find a better job inside her firm.

Her first step toward a different approach was when she started using the collaboration tools at her firm. She liked the interaction online and the ability to discover people across the company who shared her interests. When she started participating in an online community like the one Jordi used, she became interested in how to make the community better and began doing research and talking with experts. As she learned more about how to organize successful online communities, Mara shared her work so others could create their own groups. Over time, that helped her develop a reputation as an expert in communities and collaboration and led to a full-time job as the head of a collaboration team. Though still at the same firm, she went from the worst job possible to a job she genuinely loved. She noted that the process of finding the new role was unlike anything she had experienced before:

> *Usually you go through the available jobs and try to get picked for one. But I created the job. And it evolved as I learned more about what it could be. It's the complete opposite of what you normally do. It's like being able to write your own job description. You become the job. I didn't know that was possible before.*

As Mara built communities at work, learning by doing, she found she had more to say. She started to speak in public. "I didn't feel like an expert. Who am I to speak to these people? But when I talked to more people, I realized I knew more than I gave myself credit for." She went on to speak at major conferences in Paris, Sydney, and Berlin. She lectured at Imperial College in London and spoke at countless events at her firm. People at all levels recognized her as an expert. Later in the book, you'll learn how she connected with CEOs and a former prime minister as she continued to work in an open, generous, connected way. Based on her learning, her contributions, and her purposeful networking, Mara now has more possibilities than ever. She could stay at her firm, broadening her expertise by working with different businesses, or she could leverage her network to access different roles in different firms in different industries.

Barbara Schmidt feels more engaged

Barbara is one of the nicest, most generous women I've ever met. She grew up near the Baltic Sea in Lübeck, Germany. One of four children, she was the one with the traveling bug, spending nine months at a university in Texas and taking jobs in places like Milan and Brussels. When I met her, she was working in Frankfurt in a group responsible for her firm's books and records. She spent a lot of time analyzing large, complicated spreadsheets.

Barbara was one of the first people I coached, and we worked out a series of sessions that ultimately became the guided mastery program described in part III. In our first call, we tried to figure out what her goal would be. Did she want more money or recognition at work? A different job in finance? She mentioned she enjoyed helping people with taxes. Could exploring that be her purpose? None of those goals were appealing. It turned out that Barbara didn't consider herself a finance person. Though she was good at it, particularly the detailed analysis, it wasn't *her*. "I just sort of stumbled into it after university," she said, and she didn't know how or when to change. Barbara liked the job she had, but she was curious about what other options might exist, so she decided her goal would just be "to see what else is out there."

That's when we started to talk about her other interests, and the one she was most animated about was genealogy. Most people may think of genealogy as charting their family tree, but Barbara took it much further. She would spend hours poring over old church and government records. When she hit a dead end, she would call archivists for possible leads. She did this kind of research for her own family and then started doing it for historical figures and for particular dates in history. She was also writing about it regularly.

To build her network, Barbara began by simply looking for other people like her, including other bloggers, people who organized genealogy conferences, and firms that specialized in family tree research. She followed them online, exchanged e-mails and tweets, and even had some of her content featured on geneabloggers.com. That's when she discovered that people did genealogy for companies too, and that her own firm had a corporate historical society. She learned that people made a living producing corporate histories—books, documentaries, and online content. Her favorite example was a beautiful online history for a company in her hometown of Lübeck, and she contacted the person in charge. She even discovered that there were associations of archivists across Germany and the region.

The more she looked, the more she found. In her words, it was like discovering "a whole new world" of possibilities.[4] For the first time, she wondered if she could somehow connect her passion in genealogy to her work inside her firm. Maybe, for example, she could promote the work of the corporate historical society. She was nervous about contacting them but finally reached out via e-mail, describing her appreciation for their work. That led to more interactions, including organizing a corporate history event and helping them engage more people on her firm's enterprise social network.

> *Just had my call from the historical society. And it was amazing! Again I have this huge grin on my face ;) He directly asked me for my opinions regarding the examples he sent me and if I have other ideas...*[5]

Barbara went on to write that "working out loud changed my life."[6] Though she was still looking at complicated spreadsheets, collaborating with the corporate historians helped her feel like she could bring her whole self to work. She also had more control of her learning and her network, and she was routinely discovering new people, ideas, and possibilities in a way that felt purposeful.

A few months after she wrote that post, a senior manager at her firm noticed Barbara's work and asked if she would join his team. He had never met her, and it wasn't her spreadsheet or genealogy skills that attracted his attention but the way she communicated and collaborated online. He needed those skills for a new program about to launch. They spoke on the phone, and a few weeks later she moved to London to begin a new job and a new phase in her career.

Four different people. One approach.

"A better career and life" certainly means different things to these four people. They started from different places and experienced different kinds of benefits. What they have in common is their open, generous, connected approach to work and life. People like Jordi and Joyce seem to do it naturally. They were working out loud before the term was even coined and without any help from me. Others, like Mara and Barbara, just needed some help to learn new skills, develop new habits, or become more systematic in their approach.

As you'll see from the wide range of stories in the rest of the book, you too can approach work and life like Jordi, Joyce, Mara, and Barbara. You can improve your career and life in ways that matter to you.

Chapter 2

Improving Your Odds

Luck is not chance—
It's toil—
Fortune's expensive smile
Is earned.
—Emily Dickinson

My mother believed that some people were born under a lucky star and that the unlucky ones couldn't do much about it. In the parking lot of life, she figured, some people would always get the space near the entrance while others got a scratch on their bumper. But luck is not a matter of fate alone, and it's not just Emily Dickinson who wrote about that. Two thousand years ago, Seneca the Younger wrote, "Luck is what happens when preparation meets opportunity." Louis Pasteur said, "Chance favors the prepared mind." They all believed that with the right kind of effort, you could improve your odds, and experience a better career and life.

This chapter will help you understand more precisely what "better" might mean for you, including research on why we do what we do and what makes for a more optimal experience. That knowledge will guide your efforts to improve how you feel about work and about life in general, allowing you to make your own luck.

What makes some people love their jobs?

Behavioral research from the last few decades has given us greater insight into what motivates human beings as a species, and that helps us know what underpins a better career and life. It turns out that the way we relate to our work isn't correlated to the kind of job we have as much as it's correlated to our approach to our job and the environment in which we do it. Being a surgeon, for example, isn't *innately* more or less fulfilling than being a factory worker. What matters more is an individual's subjective view of surgery and factory work and the conditions in which he does it—the people, physical environment, systems, and processes.

To test this, a team of researchers surveyed people in clerical and professional jobs to understand how they viewed their work.[1] They asked people if they viewed what they did as a job, a career, or a calling. Was work just about money, about a deeper personal involvement where they marked achievement through advancement, or did they take pleasure in the work itself and the fulfillment that came from doing it? Surprisingly, people in the same role were evenly split in viewing their work in those three ways. Because the way people related to their work "could not be reduced to demographic or occupational differences,"[2] the researchers knew it must be something else that makes us view similar roles so differently.

A major factor that determines how we view our work is whether we are *intrinsically* motivated to do it, as summarized succinctly in this quote from Daniel Pink's *Drive: The Surprising Truth About What Motivates Us*:

> *We have three innate psychological needs—competence, autonomy, and relatedness. When those needs are satisfied, we're motivated, productive, and happy. When they're thwarted, our motivation, productivity, and happiness plummet.*[3]

Your drive—your motivation to do something and how you feel about doing it—is based on whether or not you're meeting these psychological needs. That's highly subjective and personal. Can you relate to your company's purpose or to the people who work there? Do you feel you're getting better at what you do? Are you in control of what you do each day or how you do it? If the factory worker taps into their drive and the surgeon doesn't, the factory worker will indeed feel better about work.

Mihaly Czikszentmihalyi is a psychologist who has researched how people experience work and life, and he summarized decades of findings in his classic book, *Flow: The Psychology of Optimal Experience*. He recognized that while "a joyful life is an individual creation that cannot be copied from a recipe," there are principles we can all apply that improve our experience at work and throughout our lives.[4]

> *What I "discovered" was that happiness is not something that happens. It is not the result of good fortune or random chance. It is not something that money can buy or power command. It does not depend on outside events, but, rather, on how we interpret them. Happiness, in fact, is a condition that must be prepared for, cultivated, and defended privately by each person.*[5]

The principles he outlined include setting our own goals, developing our skills, being more conscious of others rather than self-conscious, and being able to concentrate and be involved. Notice how these correspond to the elements of our innate drive. Czikszentmihalyi found that whether our work is low skilled or high skilled, independent or team oriented, we're more likely to experience "flow" when we tap into our drive and immerse ourselves in the activity.

How the majority of us feel about work

Unfortunately, too many of us don't tap into our intrinsic motivators at work, and as a result we don't feel good about it. This is evident in employee engagement reports like Gallup's "2013 State of the American Workplace." Gallup has surveyed more than twenty-five million US workers since the 1990s, and they assert that "70 percent of the workforce is checked out," and, even worse, people are "acting out their unhappiness and undermining others."

In a *New York Times* article, Tony Schwartz and Christine Porath described a similar study with similar results.[6] In partnership with the *Harvard Business Review*, they surveyed twelve thousand mostly white-collar workers and found the majority didn't have a connection to the company's mission at work, a sense of meaning and significance, opportunities for learning and growth, or opportunities to do what they do best. The researchers labeled the modern workplace a "white-collar salt mine." One dispirited commenter said, "I feel worse after reading these comments, because it seems to be the same everywhere."

You may feel like you're a member of this majority. I certainly did. Part of the reason so many of us feel disengaged is the way work has been designed for the last century or so. At large companies in particular, work has become increasingly dehumanized, more about processes and systems than about people. In *Humanize*, Jamie Notter and Maddie Grant described how "we run our organizations like machines"[7] and wrote about the negative consequences of a mechanical model for corporations. Think about how you've felt when you had a micromanaging boss that limited your control or when you were denied access to a new role or a learning opportunity because of your place in an organization chart. The performance review process alone is enough to make people feel bad about work. I've seen people break down in tears after a bad review, all because their manager had to pick on someone to meet her quota. Our environments at work can actively *inhibit* our drive, limiting our performance as well as the performance of the firm.

It might seem like common sense that it's in the interest of the corporation to have employees feel better about their work. There's a growing set of evidence too. The

Gallup researchers, for example, compared how individuals felt about work with the overall business performance of their firm. They found that engagement at work correlated with improved performance in *nine different work categories*, from profitability and productivity to customer satisfaction and safety.[8] When compared to the actively disengaged employees (20 percent of the workforce), the engaged staff had fewer accidents, fewer defects in their work, and even lower health-care costs. Gallup estimated the cost of actively disengaged employees at around half a trillion dollars annually. When you feel better about work, it helps both you and your firm.

There are two ways to improve your odds of feeling better about work. One way is to change your approach to your current job, increasing your sense of control, learning, and relatedness so you tap into your drive. Another way is to build a network that gives you access to other jobs—a different role, boss, company, or kind of work—where it might be easier for you to tap into your drive.

Changing your approach to your current job

The researchers who studied jobs, careers, and callings went on to interview people in a wide range of jobs, including engineers, nurses, and restaurant staff. In the resulting paper, "Crafting a Job: Revisioning Employees as Active Crafters of Their Work,"[9] they described how even people in highly prescribed jobs could make changes that would fundamentally alter their view of what they did:

> *Job crafting changes the meaning of the work by changing job tasks or relationships in ways that allow employees to reframe the purpose of the job and experience the work differently. Psychological meaningfulness of work results when people feel worthwhile and valuable at work. Thus, any actions that employees take to alter their jobs in ways that increase feelings of purpose are likely to change the meaning of the work.*[10]

A nurses' handbook, for example, might have very specific guidelines for how to do a certain procedure. But some nurses viewed themselves as patient advocates, taking extra time to inform and comfort patients and their families, and they felt better about their work as a result. Computer engineers felt better when they offered help to colleagues. The short-order cook who had to follow recipes felt better when he took extra steps to "create a product worthy of pride."[11] While some people viewed their jobs as carrying out instructions, others proactively altered aspects of the job related to learning and how they interacted with people. They crafted their jobs to tap into their own intrinsic motivators—competence, autonomy, and relatedness—and they felt better about work than those who didn't.

Even if you're not a nurse, computer engineer, or short-order cook, you can craft almost any kind of job. Barbara, for example, was still immersed in spreadsheets in her role, but she felt better about her job because her new network allowed her to bring her whole self to work. Joyce's efforts to get better at something and feel more connected made her everyday experience more pleasant. Over time, I found that even a bad day could be transformed if I did something to take control, to learn, or to deepen a relationship. Even without changing jobs, the more we all tapped into our drive, the more we had a better experience at work.

Building a network that improves your access

While you might be able to tap into your drive even in terrible conditions, it's easier to do so in some environments than others. For example, some jobs might have more opportunities for learning, or some companies might have a more nurturing, respectful culture. To increase your chances of moving to a better environment, you have to first discover those environments and then have some means of accessing them. The best way to do this is via other people.

In 1973 Mark Granovetter analyzed the flow of information through social networks, and "The Strength of Weak Ties" went on to become the most cited paper in all of social science.[12] The title was based on his assertion that people to whom we are weakly tied have different information than we normally receive because they move in different circles than our close ties. That information can be critical to us, and the example he used was finding jobs. He cited a range of studies showing that people find out about jobs through personal contacts more than any other method. Then he conducted a study of his own and found that information that led to people finding new jobs came via people they barely knew or via the contacts of those people. Though close friends and family might be more motivated to help you find a job, being able to access different information from weak ties was much more important. He noted how luck played a role in interacting with weak ties:

> *Chance meetings or mutual friends operated to reactivate such ties. It is remarkable that people receive crucial information from individuals whose very existence they have forgotten.*[13]

More than thirty years before Facebook was launched, Granovetter showed that having a larger, more diverse social network would improve your luck, increasing your knowledge about a broader set of possibilities and enhancing your ability to access them.

The practical implications of this became clear to me at a networking event at my firm. Ten people were seated at a round banquet table answering the question "How did you get your current job?" Their career paths all seemed like random walks. One recent graduate happened to attend our company's event on campus, and she wound up in an arcane business area she had never heard of before. Another person's company was acquired, and as a result she had a new boss at a new firm. My favorite was an experienced person whose prior business was shut down. He got his current job after bumping into an old acquaintance at a bar. "I sent him a note, and here I am."

All of these people were playing career roulette, hoping that they would land in a good environment.

Making your own luck

Most people I speak with understand that building a certain kind of network can give them access to a much wider range of choices. They may even realize they can change their approach to their current job and feel better about it. But few people know how to change their approach or build their network, and so they leave their career and life to chance.

You can do better. The people you'll meet throughout the book used the elements of working out loud to change their everyday experience and access more possibilities. At a minimum, they found they were meeting interesting people and enjoyed having a more open, generous mindset. Others felt like they were able to better integrate their work and life, to bring their whole self to work, and that made them feel more engaged. Many more people improved their skills and visibility, created new opportunities at work, and made it possible to discover new and rewarding careers. Once people experienced the feeling of greater control, confidence, and connectedness, it was difficult to return to their old approach. They would tell me, "I could never go back."

The benefits aren't just for the young, or for extroverts, or for the lucky ones. Everyone can improve their odds and feel better about their work and life.

Key Ideas in Part I

- Whatever your background, age, or social skills, you can learn to increase your chances of creating a better career and life.

- When it comes to how we feel about work, what matters most isn't the specific kind of job we do but how we approach our job and the environment in which we do it.

- We feel better about work and life when we tap into our innate psychological needs—competence, autonomy, and relatedness—and experience more flow moments.

- Working in an open, generous, connected way helps you tap into your innate psychological needs. A richer, more diverse network gives you access to more opportunities.

Part II

The Five Elements of Working Out Loud

Chapter 3

The Evolution of "Working Out Loud"

So, is it just blogging?

—My wife, after one of my early attempts at describing working out loud

The first time I saw "working out loud" in print was in a blog post by Bryce Williams, who has been leading innovation and collaboration efforts for years at a large pharmaceutical company. He wrote it in 2010, and his post included a simple definition:

Working Out Loud = Observable Work + Narrating Your Work[1]

This formula helped a lot of people understand that working out loud included making your finished work available to other people as well as describing your work in progress—what you're reading, whom you're meeting with, and what you're learning. When I first saw the phrase and started doing research on the topic, the benefits seemed clear to me. But explaining working out loud to others proved more difficult, and reactions were decidedly mixed:

> *"Why would I do that?"*
> *"Oh, I don't like to toot my own horn."*
> *"Why would anyone else care?"*

Even my wife was struggling with it. Although I described the other elements, like generosity and a growth mindset, she was stuck on the literal, narrow definition. After the first few months of working on the book, we were talking about it over coffee early one morning, and I took a few minutes to proudly explain what I was writing about. When I was finished, there was an uncomfortable pause before she asked me, "So, is it just blogging?"

"No," I sighed, slumping my shoulders. "It's not just blogging." Because while you could meet the original definition of working out loud by blogging or using other social media to broadcast what you're doing, there was more to it than that. I was still struggling to come up with a clear and complete description of working out loud and how it could produce the kinds of changes in your work and life like the ones I experienced.

Making "working out loud" mean much more

After that discussion with my wife, I kept experimenting with the definition. In presentations, written material, even in elevator conversations, I tried to build on Bryce's original formula while keeping it clear and simple. Early attempts were clunky:

> *Working out loud is working in an open, generous, connected way that enables you to build a purposeful social network, become more effective, and access more opportunities.*

That was accurate, but it didn't exactly roll off the tongue. So I started trying this instead:

> *Working out loud starts with making your work visible in such a way that it might help others. When you do that—when you work in a more open, connected way—you can build a purposeful network that makes you more effective and provides access to more opportunities.*

This felt a bit better, but the idea that working out loud "starts with making your work visible" was still too limiting. As I coached more people and took part in more Working Out Loud circles, I saw that working out loud has other important elements and that the elements are interrelated. For example, I saw that working out loud is most effective when you view it as a human process first and a technological one second. It's true that making your work visible amplifies who you are and what you do and that it further increases your chances of connecting with people who can help you. But it's just one of the five elements, and different people put more or less emphasis on different elements.

Working out loud even when you're not visible

I became acutely aware of this when one of the first members of a Working Out Loud circle said she didn't want to be visible. Confused, I asked her why she joined a circle in the first place, and she replied via e-mail:

> *What made me join? Wanting to be connected and feeling somewhat emotionally unconnected to work. My team is great, and I really love being here, but the work itself is fairly dry and, dare I say it, uninspiring. So I guess I wanted a bit of a shakeup to see if I could feel more engaged about work (and life in general because work is a very large part of my life).*
>
> *I'll add one more bit—while my goal itself has been deliberately not work related (I had been working for three years to get to VP and felt it was emotionally draining!), thinking about people and networks and just simple possibilities in a different way is already making me more open at and about work. I'm meeting more interesting people, and I am comfortable with the thought that the job need not be everything in life and that it is very easy to give back if I just look around.*

That e-mail stuck with me. The phrases she used to describe benefits—"making me more open" and "meeting more interesting people"—made me see that I should be focusing less on a textbook definition of working out loud and more on simple language that described both what it is and the benefits of doing it. Here's what I use now:

> *Working out loud is an approach to work and life. It helps you achieve your goals and feel better about work while you discover more possibilities.*
>
> *Think "Dale Carnegie meets the Internet." As you work out loud, you leverage principles for building meaningful relationships as well as ways to share your work, get feedback, and interact with others who share your interests. Importantly, you wrap all of this in a mindset of generosity. All that's required is a set of skills and habits that anyone can learn.*

There are five elements in this description that we'll go through in the next five chapters: purposeful discovery, relationships, generosity, visible work, and a growth mindset. For each element, you'll learn about research on why it's important, and you'll read stories of people who embody it when they work out loud. Combined, the five elements create a mindset —an open, generous, connected approach to work and life—that is the essence of working out loud. It's a mindset you'll practice developing yourself in part III.

A member of a Working Out Loud circle in the UK captured it with this beautiful illustration:

Artwork by Jon Ralphs.

Key Ideas in this Chapter

- Working out loud has five elements: purposeful discovery, relationships, generosity, visible work, and a growth mindset.

- The elements are interrelated, and people tend to emphasize different elements depending on their attitudes and aptitudes. The more you embrace each element, the more you increase your chances of making your work and life better.

- Combined, the five elements create an open, generous, and connected approach to work and life.

Exercises

Does anyone actually do the exercises in books? I didn't. But then I read *Steering by Starlight* by Martha Beck, and the exercises were so simple that I completed most of them by writing directly in the spaces provided. So in this book I tried to emulate the simplicity and practicality of Martha Beck's exercises.

Each of the remaining chapters in part II end with two exercises: something you can do in one minute and something you can do in five minutes. They're meant to be so quick and easy you can do them on your phone wherever you happen to be. You can find thc complete list of exercises at workingoutloud.com. Here are the first two.

Something you can do in less than a minute

Research cited in the last chapter showed how people in different roles were evenly split in viewing their work as a job, career, or calling. How do you view your work? Why?

Something you can do in less than 5 minutes

How many people do you know outside your firm who do what you do? Write down their names. What do you think of this list? When was the last time you exchanged information with people on it?

Chapter 4

Purposeful Discovery

"Follow your passion" might just be terrible advice.
—Cal Newport, *So Good They Can't Ignore You*

There are many possible careers in the world and an infinite number of paths through life. How do you know which ones would be better for you? Where do you start looking?

At different stages of my life, I was sure I had the answer to the question "What should I do with my life?" When I was five, I was certain I was going to be a paleontologist, digging up dinosaur bones. At eleven, I knew I would be a baseball player. As I grew older, my equally clear purposes in life were to be a psychologist, a reengineering consultant, and a computer scientist who would model how the brain works. None of that happened. Instead I spent more than twenty years working in big banks.

The sad part isn't that I didn't fulfill my early career aspirations. It's that I bought into a romantic myth of having One Special Purpose that I was never able to find or fulfill.

In *The Pleasures and Sorrows of Work*, a career counselor described the consequences of this common misconception:

> *He remarked that the most common and unhelpful illusion plaguing those who came to see him was the idea that they ought somehow, in the normal course of events, to have intuited—long before they had finished their degrees, started families, bought houses, and risen to the top of law firms—what they should properly be doing with their lives. They were tormented by a residual notion of having through some error or stupidity on their part missed out on their true "calling."*[1]

One of the major problems with identifying your true calling is that you're aware of only a tiny fraction of the possibilities, and picking solely from what you already know is grossly limiting. Even if you could identify your passion and are willing to follow it, you can't know all of the different ways to turn that passion into a career nor what that career will feel like once you do. Jordi Muñoz, for example, may have dreamed of being a pilot when he was four, but that's only because he had no idea about all the other kinds of jobs that might be better. When he was a teenager, the company he would work for and the technology it used didn't even exist yet.

At times I hoped that my path would simply manifest itself. Like the man who found his next job via a chance meeting in a bar, I relied on serendipity, those wonderful moments when things happen by chance in a beneficial way, to show me my next step. But the problem with relying on serendipity is that it is, by definition, unreliable. It leaves your happiness completely up to chance.

Instead of actively blazing a trail through life, I felt like I was on a moving sidewalk. Fortunately, I found there's a much better way to guide your decision making that will lead you to more rewarding possibilities. That better way is purposeful discovery, a form of goal-oriented exploration. You start by choosing a goal you care about and then using the different elements of working out loud to build a network of relationships, get feedback, and learn about ways to improve and about other possibilities. The goal orients your activities, and as you get feedback and learn, you adapt your goal accordingly.

Reasons to start small and adapt as you learn

Matt worked in the IT department of a big financial services firm, and he wanted a change. After considering it for some time, his idea was to combine his analytical skills with his finance experience and become a financial advisor. That seemed reasonable enough.

The first thing Matt thought to do was to get the necessary certification. Unfortunately that required passing a demanding exam, which meant a lot of study time and a fair amount of money. He asked if the firm would pay for preparation classes and for the exam fee, but his manager said no. Matt was upset that the firm wasn't willing to invest in him and saw this as a barrier he didn't know how to get past. A year later, he still hadn't made any progress toward changing his job.

Matt would have fared better if he had started with a simpler goal and used the elements of working out loud to discover more about being a financial advisor and about other related jobs. *What do advisors do all day? What's the worst part about it? What else is out there?* By sticking with a big goal and a big first step, Matt lost the opportunity over that year to learn more about his potential new field and discover other possibilities.

In contrast, Jordi's goal was simply to get better at something he loved doing. Through the work he was doing in his online community, he was able to discover different ways to improve his skills and apply them in a wider range of contexts, including at a job he could never have imagined otherwise. The same was true for Joyce, Mara, Barbara, and me. We all started with a simple goal that we cared about intrinsically. Then, in the process of building our network by making contributions to it (something you'll do yourself in part III), we learned about a range of ways to make work better. We came to understand what we liked and didn't like related to our initial goal, discovered new people and new possibilities, and refined our goal as we explored further.

Here's another example of someone who embraced purposeful discovery. His story shows how even a vague goal, when combined with the other elements of working out loud, can orient your activities and lead you to something wonderful.

Brandon Stanton turns his hobby into a mission

Brandon Stanton grew up in a suburb of Atlanta, studied history at the University of Georgia, and took his first job as a bond trader in Chicago in 2006. A few years later, in the aftermath of the financial crisis, he was laid off. So without much money and with few prospects of getting another financial job at the time, Brandon decided to try something different. He had recently purchased a nice camera and enjoyed taking photos while walking around Chicago, so he decided his goal would be to practice his hobby as he traveled around the United States. Like many thousands of people interested in photography, Brandon's first idea was to create a photo blog based on his travels in different cities:

> *My first stop was New Orleans, then Pittsburgh, then Philadelphia. Each time I arrived in a new city, I'd get lost in the streets and photograph everything that looked interesting, taking nearly a thousand photographs every day. After each day of shooting, I'd select thirty or forty of my favorite photographs and post them on Facebook. I named the albums after my first impression of each city. Pittsburgh was Yellow Steel Bridges. Philadelphia was Bricks and Flags. I had no big ambitions at the time. All I had was some vague, naive idea of making a living by selling prints of my best photos. In the meantime, I was just posting them for my family and friends to enjoy.*[2]

He had other ideas too, including plotting ten thousand street portraits on an interactive map to create a photographic census of the city. But it was only through actually doing the work, posting it publicly on Facebook, and getting feedback that he started to try other things. Along with the usual city scenes, he started taking candid street portraits. When those portraits received a favorable response, he started asking his subjects questions and including snippets of the interview with each photo.

By the time he arrived in New York in August 2010, almost all of his photographs were of people. He created a new album on Facebook and then another one. He decided to call these albums "Humans of New York." He never intended to stay in New York, but by the end of the summer, after a short trip to Chicago to collect his things, he moved back to New York for good.

Brandon's goal kept evolving. Without any formal training in photography, he gradually kept learning to take better photos while also learning how to approach people. ("At first, the rejections sting," he said.[3]) By early 2012, what started as simple online photo albums had attracted thirty thousand likes. By April of that year, it was sixty thousand, and other people started to copy his work, creating Humans of Copenhagen, Humans of Tel Aviv, and more. Such groups helped to further spread the word about Brandon and his work. By the fall of 2013, the number of Facebook fans had skyrocketed to over a million people. Brandon was still shooting photos, but now other things became possible, including the launch of a book, an "inspiring collection of photographs and stories capturing the spirit of a city," that became a number-one *New York Times* bestseller. He was named to *Time* magazine's "30 Under 30," attracting yet more attention and opening up more possibilities. Brandon reflected on how he was able to change his life in a way that was not possible before:

> *Humans of New York is an amazing story, and it's a story that could not have happened ten years ago. Without social media, I'd probably just be a quirky amateur photographer with a hard drive full of photos. I'd be cold-calling respected publications, begging for a feature. I may have even quit by now. Instead, I've discovered a daily audience of nearly a million people. Or should I say they discovered me.*[4]

With the success he was experiencing, Brandon's goal shifted again. He was starting to make money and decided early on to give some of it away, to try to do more with his photos than he had considered possible before. He described it in an online interview in 2013:

> *I don't want to "cash out" or "monetize" HONY [Humans of New York]. I like to say it publicly because I want my audience to keep me on mission. HONY print sales have raised nearly $500,000 for charity in the past six months. I want to further monetize the site for nonprofit ventures. I honestly want to "give" HONY to New York in some way.*[5]

Brandon recently turned thirty-one. His Facebook page has more than thirteen million followers, and there are millions of followers on other platforms too. His third book is coming out later this year. In the summer of 2014, he went on a fifty-day world tour of twelve countries sponsored by the United Nations that included Iran, Iraq, Ukraine, Kenya, and South Sudan. Why go to these places? "The work has a very humanizing effect in places that are misunderstood or feared." His purpose had shifted yet again, and his fans noticed it, as expressed in a comment on a photo of four women in Iraq: "You are changing the world one interview at a time. I am very grateful."[6]

Brandon's story combines all of the five elements of working out loud. He made his work visible, and the feedback on it helped him get better while also helping him develop his network. He was generous with his work, posting it freely, and also generous with the eventual proceeds from that work. Importantly, he used his initial goal as a step toward exploring a range of possibilities that might be more meaningful and fulfilling. As a result of that exploration, in just over three years, he fundamentally changed his career and life—from out-of-work bond trader to beloved photographer, author, and philanthropist.

Finding your own way toward a better career and life

Brandon's career path is not what most of us are used to. Traditionally, the way we developed our careers was similar to the way companies used to create products or services. Not that long ago, firms needed to put most of their effort into planning so they could ensure their product was right the first time. This was because it was so difficult and expensive to build things that the cost of mistakes was high. A firm typically got just one chance to plan, implement, and ship its product or service and hope they got it right. One of the many problems with this model was that they didn't know what "right" meant until other people gave them feedback, seeing or using whatever they built. Creating things was thus a risky proposition, reserved for institutions that could afford a big investment in planning and the occasional costly mistake.

Similarly, for many careers you had to decide early on what you wanted to do for a living, typically well before you knew whether your choice was a good one for you. You planned as best you could, but once you fell into a certain track, it was too expensive or difficult to try something else.

Reid Hoffman, the cofounder of LinkedIn, suggests that now we can take a different approach to developing our career. In *The Start-up of You*, he says, "The key is to manage your career as if it were a start-up business."[7]

> *Why? Start-ups—and the entrepreneurs who run them—are nimble. They invest in themselves. They build their professional networks. They take intelligent risks. They make uncertainty and volatility work to their advantage. These are the very same skills professionals need to get ahead today…*
>
> *The career landscape isn't what it used to be. Conventional career planning can work under certain conditions of relative stability, but in times of uncertainty and rapid change, it is severely limiting, if not dangerous. You will change. The environment around you will change.*

Today, start-ups embrace an entirely different model for developing products and services. It's called "lean start-up," and it aims to get feedback at the very beginning of the process, not the end.[8] Whatever product or service an entrepreneur has in mind, she first creates a minimum viable product—something that communicates the core idea but uses the fewest resources possible—and gets that in front of potential users or customers. Because producing things has become so much simpler and cheaper, modern entrepreneurs spend less time on abstract planning and much more time creating and getting feedback. Instead of one cycle for planning and implementation, they keep iterating, getting more feedback, and making adjustments each time to improve things.

Purposeful discovery is the equivalent of lean start-up for the start-up of you. It's the approach Brandon took, and it's how I discovered my own better career and life. I began with a simple goal of learning more about the way people collaborate. Then, as I met more people and got feedback on the work I was making visible, I developed new skills, learned about other possibilities, and adapted. The process itself was interesting and enjoyable, and it helped me make more informed decisions about what my next step should be.

Purposeful discovery is the model you should have in mind while you read this book and work out loud. Having a goal in mind helps you orient your activities, while the other elements of working out loud help you develop skills and a mindset that can unlock all sorts of possibilities.

Key Ideas in this Chapter

- Picking a job or career solely from what you already know is grossly limiting.
- Purposeful discovery is a form of goal-oriented exploration to guide your decision making and lead to better possibilities.
- Instead of fixating on One Special Purpose or relying on luck, pick a goal you care about and then use the different elements of working out loud to build a network of relationships, get feedback, learn about ways to improve, and discover other possibilities.
- Purposeful discovery is the equivalent of lean start-up for the start-up of you. Like a start-up, your initial goal orients your activities. As you get feedback and learn, you adapt your goal accordingly.

Exercises

Something you can do in less than a minute

Think of things you enjoy or are interested in learning more about that might serve as the basis for your purposeful discovery. Write down as many as come to mind within a minute.

Something you can do in less than 5 minutes

If you don't have a Twitter account already, create a basic one now. You can pick a photo and add other details later. Even if you never tweet yourself, having an account is a tremendous asset in purposeful discovery. It allows you to learn about and interact with a wider range of people than was ever possible before.

If you already have an account, install the Twitter app on your phone or scan your Twitter stream.

Chapter 5

Building Relationships

Social networks have value precisely because they can help us to achieve what we could not achieve on our own.

—Nicholas Christakis and James Fowler, *Connected*

Are you social?

Before you respond too quickly, the answer is yes. Whether or not you tweet or enjoy dinner parties, you're wired as a human being to be social. The people in your network influence you, and you, in turn, influence them. In *Connected*, researchers Nicholas Christakis and James Fowler show how this social influence extends to almost every part of our lives:

> *Networks influence the spread of joy, the search for sexual partners, the maintenance of health, the functioning of markets, and the struggle for democracy. Yet, social-network effects are not always positive. Depression, obesity, sexually transmitted diseases, financial panics, violence,*

and even suicide also spread. Social networks, it turns out, tend to magnify whatever they are seeded with.[1]

One of the many things that will traverse your social connections is your reputation—who you are, what you do, and how well you do it. That's why a big part of working out loud involves building a larger, more diverse network and developing more meaningful relationships with some of the people in that network.

Your network gives you access

We've known for a long time that your networks of relationships are important. It's why people join exclusive clubs and attend conferences. It's why Dale Carnegie's *How to Win Friends and Influence People* sold so many copies. When he first published it in 1936 as "a practical, working handbook on human relations," he only printed five thousand copies. It went on to sell fifteen million more. "People are frequently astonished at the new results they achieve," he wrote. "It all seems like magic."[2] Almost eighty years later, the book is still popular.

Your network, if developed properly, gives you access to knowledge, expertise, and influence. Mark Granovetter's "The Strength of Weak Ties" showed that people find jobs through their network. Ronald Burt, a sociologist and professor at the Chicago Booth School of Business, showed how people with better networks receive higher performance ratings, get promoted faster, and earn more money.[3]

How I learned what networking could be

Given all of this, why is the word "networking" tainted? For me, the idea of networking was always associated with shallow small talk at staged events where most people exchanged business cards they would never look at again. It felt fake and manipulative. Although I genuinely enjoyed talking with people, I felt uncomfortable "networking" with them. As a result, I had few meaningful relationships outside of family, friends, and the people I happened to be working with.

It wasn't until I was in my midforties that I started to understand what networking could be. The thing that completely changed my approach to networking and to relationships in general was the relationship mastery course I mentioned in the introduction.[4] Looking back, I'm still struck by my good fortune to participate in it. I had just read *Never Eat Alone* by Keith Ferrazzi, and he was giving a talk at my firm as part of a tour promoting his new book, *Who's Got Your Back?* Hundreds of people crammed into the room to hear him speak, and at the end, almost as an afterthought, he mentioned a year-long course he was piloting and offered four spots to people at our firm. That evening I wrote a note to the head of human resources to make a case for taking one of those spots, and I got in.

In the course, we learned techniques for reaching more people and expanding our network. More importantly, we discussed four mindsets that served as "the behavioral foundation" of developing richer and more meaningful relationships:[5]

Generosity: The willingness to offer something of yourself without expecting something in return.

Vulnerability: When you admit to a failing or weakness, you demonstrate trust in other people and make it easier for them to be authentic.

Candor: Being direct and honest with others shows you value them more than you value anything you might get from them.

Accountability: Doing what you say you will do—and admitting when you haven't—is another way to build trust.

We also discussed intimacy, getting to know people and genuinely caring about them. I remember my cynicism when we started talking about it. Intimacy and networking? But throughout the course, we practiced applying these concepts as we worked with each other in class and as we reached out to other people. When it came to intimacy, for example, there was an exercise over dinner in which we sat next to people we didn't know and had "forty-five minutes to care about them." We turned to each other with a look of dread and anxiety. But we did it, and more than five years later, I'm still friends with the woman I sat next to. As Keith Ferrazzi said during the class, "When you know someone, really get to know him or her as a human being, how could you not care?"

At work and at home, I started to replace small talk with conversations that showed my genuine interest in the other person. I asked more questions and became a better listener.

I was humbler and more vulnerable. The results, as Dale Carnegie wrote in 1936, seemed like magic. Instead of networking feeling shallow and manipulative, it felt authentic and helpful. I saw that making connections wasn't about collecting contacts but about building deeper, more meaningful relationships with people.

What's the best kind of network?

The authors of *Connected* showed that in addition to a network being important for transmitting information, practices, disease, and more, the *kind* of network matters. Certain types of information only pass between people who trust each other. Diseases, though, will only become epidemics if they find a way out of the initial group where the outbreak began, like someone with an infectious disease getting on a plane to a foreign country.

Over the last century, mathematicians have become increasingly interested in studying different kinds of networks, trying to come up with models that emulate our experiences with networks in the real world, including social networks. The model would have to explain how, for example, most people have a relatively small set of connections, yet in study after study there seems to be only six or so degrees of separation between any two people. How and why is that possible?

In 1998 Duncan Watts and Steven Strogatz came up with an explanation. In a short, dense paper titled "Collective Dynamics of 'Small-World' Networks," they showed how a certain kind of network would be effective at transmitting messages while also emulating our experience in real life.[6] Underlying the rigorous mathematics, a small-world network has two simple characteristics. The first is that such a network includes small clusters that are densely connected. Think of a group of five people where everyone is connected to everyone else. The second characteristic of small-world networks is that larger groups are sparsely connected. Think of two clusters, for example, with only one person in common. Researchers have discovered small-world network properties in real-world phenomena ranging from electric power grids to neural networks to social networks. Why? It seems all kinds of systems are trying to optimize the efficiency of different networks, balancing the benefits of being connected with the costs of maintaining those connections.[7]

As you build your social network, you're not trying to maximize your number of connections or even your number of deep relationships. You're trying to build a network with both strong and weak ties. You need clusters of connections who trust you so you can exchange sensitive and valuable information. You also need people who are different from you—in geography, jobs, and interests—because they'll have information and contacts you and your strong ties don't have.

Building your own small-world network

While taking Keith Ferrazzi's course, I was struggling to think of who should be in my network. But then I saw a presentation by Seth Godin that made me think more broadly about what networks are and why people join them. He referred to a certain kind of network as a tribe, "a group of people connected to one another, connected to a leader, and connected to an idea."[8] In his TED talk on tribes, he described an extraordinary array of them, from groups of people who make balloon animals to people who care about important causes and band together to make a difference.[9] Tribes are good examples of small-world networks because networks built around ideas tend to be diverse and consist of both strong and weak ties. A *Harvard Business Review* article titled "How to Build Your Network" noted that "shared activities bring together a cross-section of disparate individuals around a common point of interest, instead of connecting similar individuals with shared backgrounds."[10] Seth Godin's talk also highlighted that now, more than any time in history, it's easier to join or lead tribes you care about.

> *Geography used to be important. A tribe might be everyone in a certain village, or it might be model-car enthusiasts in Sacramento, or it might be the Democrats in Springfield...Now, the Internet eliminates geography. That means that existing tribes are bigger, but more important, it means there are now more tribes, smaller tribes, influential tribes...and tribes that never could have existed before.*[11]

The story of Jordi Muñoz is an example of that. He was able to find and connect with a diverse set of people based on his hobby. The online drones community became his tribe, and their shared interest was the desire to learn more about technology that was new and exciting to them. Without that tribe, Jordi's access to opportunities would have been limited, based on the people he knew in Ensenada or that he could have corresponded with directly.

I started to understand that my tribe didn't have to be big, nor did it need to be just about me. Instead, my network could be based on interests shared by diverse groups of people around the world. This next story shows how you can leverage a tribe related to your job to amplify your reputation and increase your access to opportunities.

Nikolay builds his tribe and shapes his reputation

Nikolay Savvinov is an engineer in Moscow who specializes in improving the performance of databases, and he's extremely good at what he does. Yet despite being one of many thousands of IT people in a large global firm, it was easy to feel isolated. The only people aware of Nikolay or his work were his manager and the few people who had to call on him for help. So Nikolay set out to change that, to have more people around the firm and around the world know who he was and what he was capable of.

To do that, Nikolay used a collaboration platform at his firm and a public blog to make his work visible and to reach more people in his tribe. At work he is one of the top contributors to an online community of approximately four hundred database experts, regularly posting technical content there that might help other engineers (e.g., "A handy utility for analyzing SQL plans"). He also organized a performance-tuning working group where others could contribute and learn from each other, and he actively looked in the community for people posting database performance problems so he could offer his assistance.

Four hundred people inside a large global company may not seem like a lot. But they are the four hundred people in the firm who matter most to Nikolay because they're precisely the people who have access to database jobs around the world. As a result of his contributions, anyone searching for "database performance" or "database community" would find Nikolay. Without even knowing his title or his manager, they would quickly see his work and know he is a leading expert in the firm for the specific engineering topic they cared about. He would be an expert not just because he said so, but because his contributions were visible and because others provided positive feedback on his work.

Nikolay is applying this same approach externally using a public blog at savvinov.com. There, he publishes insights into different aspects of his specialty, the performance tuning of Oracle databases. He even offers "free tuning help to beginners." Of course, this blog also appeals to only a specific technical niche. But consider how Nikolay has taken control of his reputation as an expert, and compare his chances of getting a job versus, say, another expert with a one-page resume. Instead of his career depending solely on his relationship with a single manager in Moscow, Nikolay has improved his chances. His online body of work, the generous and consistent way in which it's offered, along with public feedback on his contributions are all increasing his access to opportunities in case he ever wanted to make a change.

The joy of networking

The research shows that building social networks is a fundamental part of the human condition, but learning the best way to build those networks hasn't been easy. It's the behavioral foundation Ferrazzi taught, particularly generosity, that transforms networking from something that might be inauthentic or uncomfortable into something utterly different.

In part III, as you build your own small-world network, you'll experience the joy of discovering new people combined with a sense of relatedness as you deepen relationships over time, and it will give you access to learning and other opportunities. Your small-world network will make your own world bigger and richer, and you'll come to see networking as a natural means of exploring and relating, as something you do every day and that you genuinely enjoy.

Key Ideas in this Chapter

- Your network, if developed properly, gives you access to knowledge, expertise, and influence.

- Generosity, vulnerability, candor, accountability, and intimacy serve as the behavioral foundation for deepening your relationships, and they transform networking from something that might feel inauthentic to something that's fulfilling.

- Ideally your network includes clusters of strong ties with people who trust you so you can exchange valuable information as well as weak ties with people who are different from you, who have information and contacts that you and your strong ties don't have.

- Finding and connecting with your tribe—"a group of people connected to one another, connected to a leader, and connected to an idea"—is easier than ever.

Exercises

Something you can do in less than a minute

Post this on Twitter: "Reading *Working Out Loud* by @johnstepper"

By describing what you're reading, you'll be narrating your work. If you @-mention me on Twitter, I'll be alerted and will respond with my own tweet, showing you how even a simple six-word contribution can create a connection that wouldn't have been possible before.

Something you can do in less than 5 minutes

Create a LinkedIn account. Like your Twitter account, you can pick a photo and add other details later. For now, create a basic account, and use the rest of your time to skim an article on what makes a good profile.[12] If you already have an account, take a minute to install the app on your phone and review your profile.

Chapter 6

Leading with Generosity

The world is full of people who are grabbing and self-seeking. So the rare individual who unselfishly tries to serve others has an enormous advantage. He has little competition.
—Dale Carnegie, *How to Win Friends and Influence People*

Imagine you're reading this book while lazing by the pool at a fancy resort. You're alone, sipping fresh coconut water straight from the coconut, when you hear a cry for help and you realize a man is drowning. Quickly you calculate there is a fifty-fifty chance the person will die if you don't help him and a 5 percent chance you'll both drown if you attempt to rescue him. What would you do?

It turns out that we have evolved to want to save the other person. That's because if we each choose to save the drowning man, and others are likely to reciprocate (because we've evolved with similar instincts), then we all reduce our chances of drowning and will be more likely to pass on our genes.

The evolution of reciprocal altruism

The name for this behavior is "reciprocal altruism," and it isn't limited to humans. In 1937 Meredith Crawford put two young chimpanzees in a cage and showed that they are also wired to help each other under certain conditions.[1] In the experiment, a heavy box with food on top was placed outside the cage. The chimps could pull on ropes connected to the box to bring it closer and get the food, but the box was too heavy for any one chimp to pull alone. To get the food, they had to cooperate. Fairly quickly, two hungry chimps learned to pull in unison so they could both get the food. Even more interesting, when only one of the chimps is hungry, the chimp that doesn't want the food *pulls the box anyway*. Though the hungry one winds up eating everything, the other chimp helps in return for a greater chance of reciprocity in the future.

In 1971 Robert L. Trivers provided a comprehensive model for this behavior. In a fascinating paper titled "The Evolution of Reciprocal Altruism," he analyzed birds that cry out to warn of predators despite the threat of disclosing their own location.[2] He also described in detail the behaviors of fish that groom other fish despite the threat of being eaten. Groupers, for example, are large predators with simple brains relative to ours. They've evolved to take advantage of the long-term benefits of being serviced by parasite-eating cleaner fish while sacrificing the short-term benefit of an easy meal. Even after a cleaning, groupers won't eat the cleaner fish so they can preserve the likelihood of future cleanings. While we may think of the world as being a dog-eat-dog competitive environment, it can also be "cleaner fish helps grouper," and everybody wins.

Digging further into the conditions under which animals do this and with whom, Frans de Waal, a director at the Yerkes Primate Center, studied capuchin monkeys. He showed that, when given a choice, capuchins prefer helping themselves plus a partner over helping only themselves. He called that "prosocial behavior" and found that subjects systematically favored the prosocial option if their partner was familiar, visible, and fair.[3]

> *We believe prosocial behavior is empathy based. Empathy increases in both humans and animals with social closeness, and in our study, closer partners made more prosocial choices.*

The deeper the relationship with people in your network, the more likely they are to help you.

Combining the "two great forces of human nature"

When it comes to humans, we have an even greater capacity for the cognitive demands of reciprocal altruism. For example, we have a greater ability to calculate the costs and benefits of saving a drowning person. Beyond this rational capacity, we experience emotional rewards that affect the kinds of help we offer and emotional bonds that affect our choice of recipient for that help. Our system of giving and taking is much more complicated than tit for tat. Yet, like the other species who practice reciprocal altruism, we see that humans, too, can benefit individually from offering things to others. Professor Adam Grant from Wharton explored this in his book *Give and Take*. He showed how you can be both generous and purposeful:

> *Most people assume that self-interest and other-interest are opposite ends of one continuum. Yet in my studies of what drives people at work, I've consistently found that self-interest and other-interest are completely independent motivations: you can have both of them at the same time. As Bill Gates argued at the World Economic Forum, "there are two great forces of human nature: self-interest, and caring for others," and people are most successful when they are driven by a "hybrid engine" of the two. If takers are selfish and failed givers are selfless, successful givers are otherish: they care about benefitting others, but they also have ambitious goals for advancing their own interests.*[4]

You don't need to keep score or view networking as a set of transactions. Rather, you contribute to individuals in your network without expectations, knowing that, across the entirety of the network, reciprocal altruism makes it likely you will ultimately benefit too.

What do you have to offer?

The question "What do you have to offer?" seems to make even the most skilled and generous people uncomfortable. If you're cleaning a grouper of ectoparasites or saving someone who's drowning, then it's clear what it means to serve others. But applied to everyday life, the idea of serving others can seem too abstract or even naïve. As a result, many of us feel hesitant about giving even the simplest things.

The severity of the problem became clear to me one day as I sat with a former high school classmate who was looking to change jobs. As we talked, I was struck by his deep understanding of the complex business he was in, his work with many African countries, and his near encyclopedic knowledge of music. He was also married and had children, and we shared stories about our families. Talking with him was a pleasure. Yet he struggled with building his network. When I asked him about the contributions he could make to deepen relationships, he paused and looked embarrassed. Despite all his skills and experiences, he simply didn't know what to offer other people or how to offer it.

You already have valuable gifts

When Dale Carnegie wrote about the best approach to building relationships, he didn't mention wealth or highly specialized skills. His advice included things anyone could do:

Give honest and sincere appreciation.
Become genuinely interested in other people.
Talk in terms of the other person's interests.
Be a good listener.
Encourage other people to talk about themselves.
Make the other person feel important—and do it sincerely.

Keith Ferrazzi called these "universal currencies," things anyone could give and anyone would like to receive. They're simple and yet powerful. Think of the last time someone gave you specific positive feedback about your work. How did that make you feel? Or when someone trusted you enough to be vulnerable. How often does that happen? Universal currencies can be among the most valuable gifts we have to offer.

With social tools, it has become easier than ever to offer these simple gifts in addition to what you might do in person. Here are just a few examples:

- Thank someone.
- Offer public, positive feedback on work you admire.
- Connect people for their mutual benefit.

You have so much to offer, and we haven't yet mentioned skills specific to you—to your job, your education, your culture, your life experiences. This is just a start, and there will be a more complete guide to contributions in part III, including when and how to offer them. For now, the point is for you to think broadly and in a human way about all that you have to offer. Nikolay offered his help to people in his community. Jordi contributed his designs. Brandon freely posted his photos and raised a substantial amount of money too. They all led with helpful, genuine contributions, and they all benefited as a result.

Here's an example of someone who freely shares his knowledge and experience every day. Though he's already successful and wealthy, his contributions help him reach more people and gain access to even more possibilities.

Fred Wilson, venture capitalist

When it comes to leading with generosity, venture capitalists might not come to mind. But Fred Wilson is not your average venture capitalist. He's the cofounder of Union Square Ventures, a New York City–based venture capital firm whose portfolio includes Internet companies such as Twitter, Tumblr, Foursquare, Zynga, and Kickstarter. He also blogs every day.

He started when he was forty-two. During the last ten years, he's written over 6,200 posts on avc.com, attracting more than nine million unique visitors. He writes mostly about technology and technology start-ups. One series, for example, is called "MBA Mondays" and provides detailed advice to entrepreneurs on everything from hiring to employee equity to how to scale a company. But he also writes about his personal experiences, from business failures to music he likes:

> *I write every day. It is my discipline, my practice, my thing. It forces me to think, articulate, and question. And I get feedback from it. When I hit publish, I get a rush. Every time. Just like the first time. It is incredibly powerful.*[5]

Though venture capitalists normally have good networks, Fred Wilson's daily contributions allow him to reach a much broader audience. In addition to the nine million visitors, more than ten thousand people have contributed over one hundred and fifty thousand comments. The "AVC community," as Fred refers to them, has debated issues, pushed for legislation, and funded good causes. That community even led Fred to explore some very different possibilities:

> *A number of years ago, I wrote a blog post talking about the need to teach middle school and high school students how to write software. In the comments (where the good stuff happens), a Google engineer told me to go down to Stuyvesant High School and meet a teacher named Mike Zamansky who had taught him to write code in high school. So I did that and thus begun my education into the world of computer science education in the NYC public high school system. What I learned was that other than Mike's program at Stuyvesant and a few other small programs, there wasn't much. So began my quest to see more computer science and software engineering in the NYC public school system.*[6]

Fred went on to provide the initial funding for what became the first Software Engineering Academy in downtown New York City, and he's an increasingly vocal, visible advocate for education.

Giving as a way to make work and life better

Another venture capitalist who shares the perspective of Fred Wilson is Reid Hoffman. In an insightful article titled "Connections with Integrity," he described why leading with generosity is important:[7]

> *I believe that the people who tend to become more effective in the world are those who build and nurture the best alliances.*
>
> *One way to help nurture good alliances is to provide early and explicit signs of your own commitment, showing people that you actually care about helping them. My name for this practice is the "theory of small gifts." There are many small ways to invest in a relationship and create more value for everyone, without expecting anything tangible in return. For example, you can offer to introduce people to others in your network; if the introduction is well chosen, it can be one of the most valuable things you can do for someone...*
>
> *It seems counterintuitive, but the more altruistic your attitude, the more benefits you will gain from the relationship. If you insist on a quid pro quo every time you help others, you will have a much narrower network and a more limited set of opportunities. Conversely, if you set out to help others...simply because you think it's the right thing to do, you will rapidly reinforce your own reputation and expand your universe of possibilities.*

Reid Hoffman, Keith Ferrazzi, and Dale Carnegie aren't pure altruists. They all ran successful businesses, fully aware that they have a limited amount of resources. But like all the different species who practice reciprocal altruism, they understood that certain gifts, freely given, increased their own long-term chances for success. That's why generosity is an element of working out loud and why Keith Ferrazzi wrote, "the currency of real networking is not greed but generosity."[8] Since you won't know which individuals in your network will help you in the future, you lead with generosity and empathy in all of your interactions.

Key Ideas in this Chapter

- Self-interest and other-interest are completely independent motivations: you can have both of them at the same time.
- You already have the most valuable gifts there are to offer.
- Even Fred Wilson, who was already wealthy and successful, found he could build a more diverse network and access more possibilities through his contributions.
- It seems counterintuitive, but the more altruistic your attitude, the more benefits you will gain from the relationship.

Exercises

Something you can do in less than a minute

Show public appreciation on Twitter for someone's work. Don't expect to get a reply. Do it just because it's a nice thing to do, and if someone does reply, that's a bonus. Below, for example, I shared how much I was enjoying reading *The Happiness Project*, an excellent book by Gretchen Rubin. I admit to being thrilled when she responded.

Public feedback isn't intimate (it's public, after all), but it's still a lovely gift. It shows you want others to know someone has done something worth your gratitude. Just make sure the gift is pure and really about the recipient, not about you.

Something you can do in less than 5 minutes

E-mail someone now to say "thank you." Then send a LinkedIn message to someone else to say "I've been thinking of you and hope you're well."

These are private messages and thus more personal. Notes like these are simple, universal gifts that anyone would like to receive. You can add other details if you like, but keep these notes to no more than a few sentences.

Chapter 7

Making You and Your Work Visible

Sharks in Western Australia
are now tweeting out where they are.
—Alan Yu, "More Than 300 Sharks in Australia Are Now on Twitter"

Of the twenty fatal shark attacks around the world in 2011 and 2012, six of them were in Australia, prompting researchers there to find better ways of making the presence of sharks more visible to swimmers in the area.

So they put the sharks on Twitter.

Not that long ago, the only way swimmers would know if a shark was around was if a person nearby spotted one and yelled "Shark!" But waiting until someone within earshot sees a big dorsal fin is both scary and ineffective. You need a better way to know when a shark is around and a better way to spread the word so you can reach a wider audience.

That led the researchers to tag hundreds of sharks with transmitters. Now whenever one of the tagged sharks comes within a half a mile of the beach, it triggers an alert to the thirty thousand followers of the Surf Life Saving Western Australia Twitter feed, noting the shark's breed and approximate location. This group, along with other beach safety and shark conservation groups (such as Shark Spotters in South Africa), also rely on humans at specific monitoring lookouts to find sharks and use Twitter to spread the word.

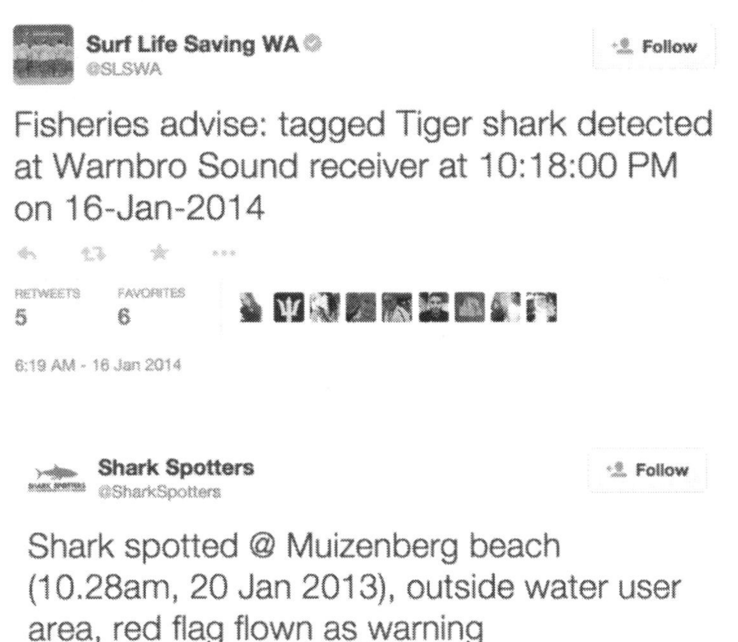
Surf Life Saving WA
@SLSWA
Follow

Fisheries advise: tagged Tiger shark detected at Warnbro Sound receiver at 10:18:00 PM on 16-Jan-2014

RETWEETS 5 FAVORITES 6

6:19 AM - 16 Jan 2014

Shark Spotters
@SharkSpotters
Follow

Shark spotted @ Muizenberg beach (10.28am, 20 Jan 2013), outside water user area, red flag flown as warning #BeSharkSmart

RETWEETS 13

12:29 AM - 20 Jan 2014

If sharks can do it...

The point of the shark story is to demonstrate how absurdly easy it is to be visible online. You can choose not to be visible, of course, and there are certainly people who have a good career and life without using social tools. Also, the use of Twitter and other social tools doesn't eliminate the need for human beings to talk to each other. If you're swimming near me and see a shark, please yell "Shark!" before you tweet it. But using social tools can further amplify who you are and what you do, expanding the set of possibilities for your network and your career. Used effectively, our interactions on social tools complement the fundamentals of relationships that Dale Carnegie and Keith Ferrazzi wrote about, significantly extending our reach.

In this chapter, I purposefully chose examples based on my experience of using these tools inside a large global firm. They show how making yourself and your work visible can help people solve problems, innovate, and generally feel better about what they do every day. While working out loud provides a wide range of personal benefits, it can yield valuable corporate benefits too.

Social tools are increasingly being used for work

Social tools include online communities, blogs, Twitter, Facebook, collaboration platforms inside firms, and a growing list of technologies that are helping people be visible and make connections. As the tools change, so will the trade-offs between them, but the principles you'll apply in using them will remain the same for a long time. Some of these tools, like the online community that Jordi used and the collaboration platform that Nikolay, Mara, and I used, have some very real functional advantages over other tools. They let you have access to deep, structured expertise (e.g., Wikipedia) *and* have access to flows of easy-to-skim information that make it easy to discover people and knowledge (e.g., Twitter). We've had this combination on the Internet since about 2006, and now we're starting to have it inside companies too.

In 2009 Andrew McAfee wrote *Enterprise 2.0* describing how firms were starting to leverage tools and practices from the Internet. In *Harvard Business Review*, he described "how to use these tools to simultaneously advance your own work, make your existence and expertise better known throughout a digital community, and benefit the organization as a whole."[1] Around that same time, more people started writing about "narrating your work"[2] and "observable work."[3] It was late in 2010 that the phrase "working out loud" appeared in a business context in the post by Bryce Williams.[4] By the end of that year, there were more software companies selling social collaboration tools and more companies buying them.

Since *Enterprise 2.0* appeared, I've been implementing social tools at a global company to change how tens of thousands of my colleagues work. Our early efforts failed. An enthusiastic minority might use a given tool, perhaps, but the majority would avoid it, dismiss a given tool as "Facebook for work," or simply not know what to do. Even those who were comfortable using social media struggled to use the social tools to help them meet a goal. They relegated the tools to purely personal use and didn't think to apply them to their everyday work.

Significantly improving how people get things done

Over several years though, we gradually learned how to realize the potential of these platforms in ways that were more convenient and comfortable for more people. To make our case to skeptical employees, one of the first things we learned was to stop using the word "social" and talk instead about the work that individuals and teams did every day. We would start with some facts about the most common tools they were already using: e-mail and meetings. Here are some statistics we would share:

- Professionals, managers, and salespeople spend 28 percent of their time reading or writing e-mail.[5]
- They spend another 19 percent of their time trying to track down information.[6]
- People check their e-mail thirty-six times per hour.[7]

Most people could recognize themselves in these statistics, and they could see how changing those numbers would be good for them as well as the firm. Not only was their individual time filled with interruptions and low-value activities, but the knowledge of the firm wasn't being captured anywhere except in people's inboxes. That knowledge couldn't be searched or built on by others in the firm, and it effectively evaporated when the person left. It's not an exaggeration to say "e-mail is where knowledge goes to die."[8]

Then we would talk about alternatives. Even if the majority of people at work may not be comfortable blogging or tweeting, everybody works. They create documents and presentations, organize meetings, attend events, and work on projects. They learn from books, classes, and colleagues. So we would show how social tools could make all of that visible and more useful. Until fairly recently that was too difficult to do. The value of sharing your work was outweighed by the effort it took both to publish it and to get it in front of people who might be interested. Now the ease of publishing combined with the ease of finding and consuming information makes it simpler than ever to make your work visible in a way that's helpful to others. It isn't about giving you yet more tasks or lumping social stuff onto your already crowded to-do list. Now making work visible can be a part of what you naturally do every day.

Real benefits of making work visible in a big firm

In 2012 we introduced a popular social collaboration platform in our firm.[9] The software is designed especially for corporations, and it allows you to write and store documents, create groups and websites, start discussions, create events, and more. You can also comment and like almost anything and see all of your updates in a stream of activity similar to Facebook or Twitter. Thousands of companies now use software like this, and it's becoming increasingly common as firms seek to modernize how their employees communicate and collaborate.

In just over two years, fifty thousand people at our firm were regularly using the social platform, and the number kept going up. Some employees used it just to search for information. Others used it as a more convenient way to share work with their team. Each month we would interview someone who was actively making his work visible and ask why he did it and how work changed for him. The benefits fell into four main categories:

- Becoming more visible
- Getting useful feedback
- Becoming more efficient
- Enjoying work more

Becoming more visible

Jennifer summed up the feelings of most people when she said, "The platform made it easier to connect with people who I might not have connected to otherwise and to get information and inputs from new places." Will, who worked in another area of the firm, said, "Using the platform introduced me to a lot of individuals across product lines and helped me to understand more about different areas of the business. You get to see a lot of talent across the division you might not have seen otherwise."

People found that making their work visible helped them shape their reputation with a wider audience. Andreas in Germany noted, "Within my regular contacts, I was regarded for my expertise. However, I wasn't recognized by my indirect managers or anyone else with whom I had no direct contact." He was asked by his manager to "show more presence," and by using the platform to respond to questions and help people, he was able to do exactly that. "I was engaged in global discussions and able to help people with my expertise."

Getting useful feedback

An executive who was already an effective communicator found she could extend her reach and get valuable feedback compared to using more traditional channels like e-mail. "Once we were on the social platform, we started reaching a wider audience and getting tremendous feedback. It's extraordinary the people I've come across as a result of working out loud." For some, the feedback they received helped improve their work. A team that made their work visible on the collaboration platform said, "We went from the attitude 'be careful how you use it' to using it under certain circumstances to insisting that everyone use it to engage with our stakeholders." The reason is that it made their work better:

> *The number of different perspectives you can get on the problems you're trying to solve is always going to lead you to a better decision...It has improved the quality of our work because of the feedback sought and provided via the platform. In addition, working out loud really helps drive a collaborative and merit-based performance culture—it*

makes it far easier for the team to see what everyone is working on and to contribute to others' objectives.

Becoming more efficient

We expected these benefits and were happy to see people realizing them. But we wanted more. We wanted to help people make their work more efficient. So we were gratified to talk to Michelle and hear that "once you're connected with people and groups that are of value to you, you can see what's happening, which can help you in your role." For her, it wasn't just about *more* connections but about connections with relevant people who could help her get better at her job. Alun described how he used to e-mail spreadsheets around and juggle multiple updates from multiple people. Now, by sharing his work online, everyone could see what had been updated and what hadn't. "An arduous process had been made more efficient, and it also has the benefit of being visible to everyone involved. My manager can go to one place and see the whole status and when it was last updated. He doesn't need to call me to chase down an answer. It's all right there."

In Nikolay's community as well as other role-based communities, we routinely saw experts coming together to solve problems and make improvements to processes. Because that was all visible, others could easily find it and build on it.

Enjoying work more

The fourth category of benefits surprised me. Some people—not everyone, but certainly a critical mass of people—started to like work more. I liked work more too, but I thought it might be because I had stumbled onto some particularly gratifying work. Others found different reasons, including that it made work easier, and it felt good to connect with people around the firm. My favorite reaction was from Derek, who posted this after having an epiphany of sorts about the power of making his work visible:

> *The best thing I have seen from the firm in my twenty-six years here.*
>
> *I knew about the platform and maybe visited it a few times but certainly never posted. I didn't think I needed to. Just how wrong can one person be? After a fairly blunt conversation with my manager, I realized I needed to "sell" myself more…In the twenty-six years I have been employed here, I have worked in a number of roles in a few different countries and never thought anyone who needed my skills didn't know who I was. Once again, I was wrong.*
>
> *So, blunt conversation fresh in my mind, let's "sell" myself. I thought about how I could do this and of course came across the social platform.*
>
> *I soon came to realize that it isn't about selling yourself, it's about everything.*
>
> *In the three or four weeks I've been using it regularly…*

- *I've helped some people out.*
- *I've contributed to conversations from people I don't (or didn't) know.*
- *I've made friends (I've got twenty-six followers currently).*
- *I've got some new LinkedIn connections.*
- *I've publicized some vendor information relevant to my job.*
- *I am following thirty-five people, and I feel like I know people now.*

Did I sell myself? I think I did but in a nice way. I certainly feel like I am contributing to the firm more, and other people know who I am and what I can offer the firm.

Paul has more impact, recognition, and fun at work

Paul is someone who experienced all of these benefits. When he started using the social collaboration platform, he was in his midforties, working in a communications group. Paul's the kind of person who doesn't talk about himself and isn't an active user of social media. He just began by posting material related to his projects, such as ways to make the firm's intranet less expensive. His intended audience was an online community of communications people analogous to Jordi's online drone community. At first a few people provided support, suggestions, and referrals to other people who might be interested. Then each time someone commented or liked his proposals, more people became aware of Paul and his work.

Whenever someone helped him, Paul would use the collaboration platform to publicly recognize the person and her contribution, further spreading the word and motivating people to help him even more. Within a few months, he had built a small online movement that saved his firm over $500,000. "I probably got this done ten times quicker than I might have through traditional channels," he said. More and more people at work, including a managing director from another division, became aware of Paul through his work online. "I know you," people would say when they met him. "Your name keeps coming up."

> *Looking back, it's actually been a great way to get "known." I now have people proactively reaching out to me because they've heard my name attached to the project. On our collaboration platform, you can create a personal brand for yourself.*

His personal brand wasn't based on spin or clever marketing of himself but on his work and the value other people saw in it. His ability to build a network and solicit feedback and ideas made him more effective at his job. Based on all of this, Paul was asked to take on additional responsibilities that went well beyond his original role. His team even won an industry award for their innovative approach, expanding his reputation outside the firm.

More people finding ways to make their work visible

Most of the examples in this chapter are based on using a collaboration platform inside an organization. But what if you don't work inside a big firm? Or what if your firm doesn't have such a collaboration platform yet? In *Show Your Work: The Payoffs and How-To's of Working Out Loud*, Jane Bozarth shows the extraordinary variety of ways that ordinary people make their work visible. Some showed finished products, but many narrated their work in progress. The book includes examples from doctors, dentists, software developers, teachers, and even topiary gardeners. Many of their contributions fell into two simple categories: *This is how I did that* and *This is what I did and why.*[10] They made their work visible, often including mistakes and lessons learned, so others in their tribe could benefit from their experience.

Just how much you share and with whom you share it is up to you. The point is that it's easier and more commonplace than ever, and it provides you with substantial benefits. Making your work visible seeds your network, allowing it to amplify who you are and what you're capable of, greatly extending your reach. That multiplies your possibilities.

Key Ideas in this Chapter

- The point of the shark story is to demonstrate how absurdly easy it is to be visible online.

- The interesting part isn't the technology but the benefits people were experiencing from using the technology. They made more connections, improved the quality of their work, became more efficient, and enjoyed work more.

- When people make their work visible, some show finished products and many narrate their work in progress. *This is how I did that. This is what I did and why.*

- You don't have to be online, but your online presence extends your reach, multiplying your possibilities.

Exercises

Something you can do in less than a minute

Google yourself. It's called a "vanity search," and people do it all the time. Wherever you happen to be now, use your phone or favorite Internet device to find yourself. Are the results you're looking at what you would like others to see? How much of your best work is visible?

Something you can do in less than 5 minutes

A few years ago, I searched for myself on the Internet and was disappointed to find an old article about some work I did and some stepper exercise equipment. Search for me now, and you'll see work I'm proud of.

Search for people you find particularly interesting, people whose work you admire as opposed to celebrities. What's their online presence like? Is it easy to find them and their work?

Chapter 8

A Growth Mindset

Self-efficacy: The extent or strength of one's belief in one's own ability to complete tasks and reach goals.
—Wikipedia

This final element, a mindset of improvement, is the most important one for making working out loud sustainable. There are three reasons for this:

1 A focus on *getting better* versus *being good* reduces the fear normally associated with trying to improve your work or relationships, enabling you to do and learn more.
2 Over time your improved capabilities give you a sense of confidence that makes further improvement more likely. That enables you to make more valuable contributions.
3 As you seek to improve yourself, you share your learning with others so they can also benefit. That reinforces the element of generosity.

To begin to understand how to develop an effective, sustainable approach to growing and improving yourself, it turns out we can all learn a lot from a group of ten-year-olds.

Focusing on learning makes a dramatic difference

Researchers Carol Dweck and Claudia Mueller from Columbia University worked with fifth-graders in a small midwestern US town and several cities in the northeast to understand the effects of different kinds of praise on motivation.[1] In one study in the late 1990s, they gave children three sets of problems: an easy set, a very difficult set, and another easy set. After the first set, all students were individually told they solved at least 80 percent of the problems they answered no matter what their actual score was. Some students were praised for their ability ("You must be really smart!"), and some were praised for their effort ("You must have worked really hard!"). Then the researchers asked each child a range of questions, such as how much they enjoyed working on the problems and the kind of problems they would prefer to see in the next set.

The second set of problems was difficult, and the children were all told they performed "a lot worse," solving no more than half of them. The researchers again asked the children about the kinds of problems they would prefer and whether they would want to work on more of them. They also asked them why they thought they didn't do as well on the second set. Was it that they didn't work hard enough, weren't good enough at those problems, or didn't have enough time? Finally the children worked on a third set of problems that was as easy as the original set.

The researchers aimed to measure whether the different kinds of praise after the first set of problems would affect how the children dealt with the setback in the second set. Would they perform differently on the next set? Would they choose easier problems? Would they view themselves differently?

The results, replicated in numerous studies, showed dramatic differences in performance. Children praised for being smart did 25 percent *worse* on the third set of problems compared to the first. Children praised for working hard performed 25 percent *better*. That's an incredible difference in performance. Even more fascinating were the other differences they found. The children praised for intelligence equated their performance with their ability. So they did all they could to maximize their performance relative to other children. They chose easier problems, asked about the performance of others, and even "misrepresented" their scores more than the other children. They had a fixed mindset, tending to describe intelligence as a trait you're born with and can't change much.

Children praised for their effort, however, equated their performance with how hard they worked. So they did all they could to maximize their learning. They chose problems that were harder and increased their learning. They were more interested in other strategies for solving the problems than in the scores of other students. They had a growth mindset, believing intelligence was something they could improve.

As you practice working out loud in part III, you want to be like the children praised for their effort. You want to have a growth mindset. You're not innately good or bad at building a network, at making your work visible, or at leading with generosity. You're just at a particular point in the process of learning, the process of getting better. That's true whether you're learning to work out loud, to design drones, or to capture more compelling photos and stories. No matter what skill you're trying to develop, you'll make more progress with less anxiety if you frame your improvement as a learning goal, worrying less about how good you are right now and focusing instead on getting better over time.

A method for getting better at anything

Albert Bandura, the most cited psychologist alive today, developed a method he called "guided mastery" that's incredibly effective for developing new capabilities. It's also the basis for part III, where you'll learn to work out loud toward a personal goal. In the 1960s, Bandura used this method to cure people of snake phobias in less than a few hours. Subjects would receive treatment combining "graduated live modeling with guided participation."[2] First they would watch for fifteen minutes through a one-way mirror as the experimenter interacted with a snake. After the snake was back in its glass cage, the subject might enter the room and sit on a chair at varying distances from the cage. Gradually the experimenter would model more and more interactions and help the subject follow along. It was the subjects who, based on their apprehensiveness, set the pace at which they proceeded. As they made progress overcoming their phobia, they noticed other changes too:

Having successfully eliminated a phobia that had plagued them for most of their lives, a number of subjects reported increased confidence that they could cope effectively with other fear-provoking events. As one subject explained it, "My success in gradually overcoming this fear of snakes has contributed to a greater feeling of confidence generally in my abilities to overcome any other problem that may arise. I have more faith in myself."[3]

That feeling, in short, is one of high self-efficacy, a strong belief that you can accomplish a task or goal. People with such a belief, like the fifth-graders in the study above, experience a wide range of benefits:

A strong sense of efficacy enhances human accomplishment and personal well-being in many ways. People with high assurance in their capabilities approach difficult tasks as challenges to be mastered rather than as threats to be avoided. Such an efficacious outlook fosters intrinsic interest and deep engrossment in activities. They set themselves challenging goals and maintain strong commitment to them. They heighten and sustain their efforts in the face of failure. They quickly recover their sense of efficacy after failures or setbacks. They attribute failure to insufficient effort or deficient knowledge and skills that are acquirable. They approach threatening situations with assurance that they can exercise control over them. Such an efficacious outlook produces personal accomplishments, reduces stress, and lowers vulnerability to depression.[4]

People who work out loud report this same feeling of self-efficacy. In developing the habit of regularly contributing to their network, they become more effective, more connected, and more confident. Joyce, for example, was able to model what others were doing with social media, try things herself, and gradually develop a sense that she too could do it. Jordi got the benefits of guided mastery by seeing what others did, submitting his own drone designs, and getting feedback on how to improve them. Now, more than four decades after Bandura's work, millions of people are using a modern kind of guided mastery to increase their self-efficacy while they get better at everything from art history to Python programming.

A modern form of guided mastery helps kids learn

In 2004 Salman Khan, a hedge fund analyst in Boston with three degrees from MIT and a Harvard MBA, started tutoring his young cousins in New Orleans. To supplement their lessons, he posted some videos on YouTube, and his cousins told him they preferred the videos over talking to him live because they could watch them at their own pace and at convenient times. To his surprise, other students stumbled onto the videos and posted comments about how helpful they were, so Khan kept recording lessons on a wider range of topics.

Over time, the audience grew and provided more feedback on what was working and not working. Salman Khan's goal shifted from helping his cousins to helping kids around the world, and Khan Academy was born. He persisted, posting hundreds and ultimately thousands of lessons. As the library grew, so did the audience and so did the number of opportunities. His work started to attract the attention of teachers and others interested in improving education. To complement the videos, Khan Academy eventually produced software that helped students know how well they were doing and where they needed help. Then for classrooms that use Khan Academy, they created dashboards for teachers too. Kids would watch lectures before class, freeing teachers to focus their in-class time on coaching customized for each child based on the data in the dashboard. More feedback led to more ideas and improvements, such as the ability for other students to become coaches and earn points and badges in the process. The teachers got feedback on their work too, so they could also improve.

Below is an excerpt from the Khan Academy vision statement. Notice how the phrases echo Bandura's description of guided mastery for both the student and the teacher.

Our vision for Khan Academy in the classroom includes:

- *Individualizing learning by replacing one-size-fits-all lectures with self-paced learning*
- *Taking a mastery-based approach to learning critical knowledge and skills (every student takes as long as he/she needs to learn each concept fully)*
- *Creating collaborative learning environments with students solving problems together and tutoring one another*

- *Using focused coaching by the teacher to address students' individual needs*
- *Providing guidance to the teacher through real-time metrics and reporting on student performance*[5]

Sitting in his hedge fund office, it would have seemed impossible for Salman Khan to create a global online education movement. But by now the pattern is familiar. He had a modest goal. He made his work visible and framed it as a contribution. Those contributions led to new connections and feedback that made his work better, and that led to him making more contributions and connecting with more people. Combined, his increased effectiveness and a bigger, better network led to more possibilities.

On YouTube alone, Khan Academy now has almost two million subscribers and five hundred million views of their library. In 2011 Salman Khan told his story in a TED talk. Bill Gates joined him on stage at the end, applauding his work and telling the audience, "It's amazing. I think you just got a glimpse at the future of education."

Creating a growth mindset

Just as Bandura saw improvement in a wide range of people, so did Salman Khan, further reinforcing that guided mastery could help anyone get better. He saw in students what Carol Dweck and Claudia Mueller saw in their fifth-grade research subjects: focusing on improvement instead of performance can make a huge difference in effectiveness and confidence over time:

> *There's a group of kids who've raced ahead, and there's a group of kids who are a little bit slower. And in a traditional model, if you did a snapshot assessment, you said, "these are the gifted kids," "these are the slow kids"...But when you let every student work at their own pace—and we see it over and over and over again—you see students who took a little bit of extra time on one concept or the other, but once they get through that concept, they race ahead. And so the same kids you thought were slow, you now would think they're gifted.*[6]

You can experience this same pattern as you work out loud. Put in terms of guided mastery, you can readily come into contact with experts modeling the work you're trying to get better at. You'll make your work visible in small steps and get feedback on that work, making progress at your own pace. All the while, you'll be strengthening your self-efficacy. But all of this hinges on you believing that you can develop new skills and habits, that you have a mindset of getting better. Following a process of guided mastery for one goal—whether you're overcoming a phobia or the challenges of trigonometry—will give you confidence to attempt other goals.

How do you develop such a mindset? Heidi Grant Halvorson, who was a graduate student at Columbia when the experiments were done with the fifth-graders, went on to conduct her own experiments and write an extremely useful book called *Succeed: How We Reach Our Goals*. She listed five ways to shift your mindset:

1. Give yourself permission to make mistakes.
2. Ask for help when you run into trouble.

3. Focus on your own progress instead of comparing yourself to others.
4. Think in terms of progress, not perfection.
5. Examine your beliefs and, when necessary, challenge them.[7]

That last one is perhaps the most fundamental. Study after study has shown how labels applied to you (by you or by others) can become self-fulfilling prophecies that unnecessarily limit what you can achieve. So you need to be on the lookout for such self-limiting beliefs and get in the habit of challenging them.

> *Whether it's intelligence, creativity, self-control, charm, or athleticism—the science shows our abilities to be profoundly malleable. When it comes to mastering any skill, your experience, effort, and persistence matters a lot...So the next time you find yourself thinking, "But I'm just not good at this," remember: you're just not good at it yet.*[8]

Thirty-one years after the snake phobia study, Bandura wrote "Cultivate Self-Efficacy for Personal and Organizational Effectiveness" in which he showed how guided mastery at work enhanced not only self-efficacy but emotional well-being, satisfaction, and level of productivity.[9] When you work in a way that's more open, generous, and connected, your work can be much more than a job. It can be an integral part of a richer life.

If you develop the habits described in part III, you too can realize these benefits and earn Fortune's expensive smile.

Key Ideas in this Chapter

- Focus on getting better instead of being good. Research on fifth-graders showed how emphasizing improvement instead of performance can make a significant difference in effectiveness and confidence.

- Guided mastery—gradual, self-paced practice in which you model others and get feedback along the way—is an incredibly effective process for developing new capabilities.

- Whether you're overcoming a phobia or the challenges of trigonometry, following a process of guided mastery for one particular goal will give you confidence to attempt other goals.

- The next time you find yourself thinking, "I'm just not good at this," remember: you're just not good at it *yet*.

Exercises

Something you can do in less than a minute

Think of three things you read recently that helped you learn something. Now use Twitter to search for the people who wrote those things and follow them.

Something you can do in less than 5 minutes

Subscribe to at least one blog. For posts related to the book, there are weekly blog posts at workingoutloud.com, and I also keep a personal blog at johnstepper.com. I particularly like subscribing to Seth Godin's daily posts at sethgodin.typepad.com and Fred Wilson's at avc.com. You can learn more about the different ways to subscribe by searching for "subscribing to a blog."

Part III

Your Own Guided Mastery Program

Chapter 9

New Habits and a New Mindset in 12 Weeks

The secret of getting ahead is getting started.
The secret of getting started is breaking your complex overwhelming tasks into small manageable tasks, and starting on the first one.
—Mark Twain

Do you remember the movie *300*? It depicted the Battle of Thermopylae in 480 BC where, in a mountain pass, three hundred Spartans stood their ground against more than a hundred thousand Persians for three full days. In addition to the extraordinary story, the movie was famous for the physical conditioning of the male actors. The lead actor, Gerard Butler, and all the other men in the film had lean, chiseled bodies that appealed to a wide audience and helped the film gross over $450,000,000 worldwide.

At the time, all the men I knew, including me, were envious. We wanted bodies like that. We were amazed to learn that all the actors achieved their physiques in just eight to twelve weeks. Even better, all the information about the workouts they did was online. Any of us could follow the instructions and have the body we said we wanted.

None of us did.

Why not? It was too much, too soon. The workouts were described as "brutal." There were even health warnings. As much as we thought we'd like to sport physiques like those we saw in the movie, we never moved a muscle.

Touching the treadmill

Martha Beck, "America's most famous life coach," routinely works with people who have personal development goals but are unable to make meaningful progress. Even a simple, practical goal like "I want to get in shape" can be problematic. We may have negative associations with the effort required to get in shape. "I hate exercise." We may not believe we're capable. "I'm not an exercise person." We may not have the knowledge or the environment we need. "I just don't have the time!"

Any of these is enough to stop you from making much progress. Combined, you won't get off the couch. What Martha Beck taught me was to break down the goal and begin with a small step so simple that it verges on ridiculous. Can't go for a run four times a week for an hour? Try once a week. Still too much? Go for five minutes. Not working for you? Walk to the treadmill and touch it every day.

Touching the treadmill won't improve your cardiovascular function, but it will make it possible to bypass your hardwired aversion to change. Early in the history of human beings, major changes were a threat. When we would see a saber-toothed tiger, the blood would flow to the base of our brain, which regulates our fight-or-flight mechanisms. The thinking parts would practically shut off. Even today, our bodies react that same way when faced with big, audacious goals. Seth Godin refers to it as "the lizard brain." Steven Pressfield calls it "the resistance." It's a common and natural reaction to change. The more evolved part of your brain really does want you to achieve your goals—to develop new capabilities that can make life richer (and longer)—but the part of our brains we carry with us from long ago is trying to protect us.

So whether it's getting in shape or working out loud, we have to reframe our goals in ways that make them less scary and that don't activate our fight-or-flight mechanism.

A guided mastery program for working out loud

Before I started writing this book, I tried a variety of techniques to help people change how they work: creating helpful guides, conducting individual one-hour sessions, organizing meet-ups, even teaching a three-month course. None of this produced as much change as I had hoped. Though people understood the concepts and liked the *idea* of working out loud, it was just too hard for them to change their habits.

Looking back, my teaching was often the verbal equivalent of handing out live snakes in a roomful of people with snake phobias. Not very helpful. Telling people they had to develop a new way of working put them on the defensive even when they agreed. Finally I realized people needed more than verbal persuasion to change; they needed practical assistance. That's when I tried coaching a few individuals over a longer period of time. We would meet one on one every week for twelve weeks, and I would help them apply the five elements of working out loud, starting off with simple steps and gradually moving on to more advanced techniques when they were ready. Just as Albert Bandura used guided mastery to cure people of their phobias and increase people's sense of self-efficacy, I was using guided mastery to help people work out loud.

It worked. People were shocked at their own ability to connect with anyone anywhere at any level—and then deepen those relationships. They saw how their expanded network unlocked access to opportunities, giving them more control of their career and life and improving the odds of reaching their goal. Mara, exuberant after connecting with the former prime minister of New Zealand, told me, "It's like magic!"

In addition to being delighted at their successes, they were surprised at how they enjoyed the process. Their previous attempts at networking were all tinged with a bad aftertaste. Now though, because they were authentic and focused on contribution, they were positive about what they were doing. They also replaced their prior ad hoc efforts with a simple, sustainable system they could go through week after week. Gradually they all developed a set of habits and mindsets that would serve them well as they pursued other goals.

Your own 12-week program

Since people make progress at different rates, the techniques, adjustments, and exercises from the 12-week program aren't mapped to specific weeks but rather to four levels of mastery: getting started, connecting, creating, and becoming a linchpin. Some people may spend three to four weeks getting started while others breeze through that first level. Some may use the whole twelve weeks creating and sharing original work while others enter that level only toward the end.

To get the most out of part III, I suggest you read it straight through just as you read the first two parts. Then, when you've finished the book, find a friend, mentor, or someone else you trust, and go through the exercises together over twelve weeks. The peer support and mutual accountability will greatly increase your chances of succeeding. Better still, form a Working Out Loud circle, a group of two to five people who meet once a week for twelve weeks. More information on how to form a circle and facilitate the weekly meetings is at the end of the book and at workingoutloud.com.

To get better results than I got after watching *300*, remember to have a growth mindset and frame the entire process as a learning goal. Whenever you hear your lizard brain talking about all the reasons you won't succeed, lull it back to sleep by telling it you're just trying to get better. Remind yourself that there's nothing to fear, really. Over twelve weeks, you'll try some new things, discover new people and ideas, and gradually develop a new set of habits that are quite pleasant. You may change your life, but by that time the lizard won't be able to stop you.

Key Ideas in this Chapter

- You have a hardwired aversion to change, even to changes that may be positive for you in the long run.

- To avoid triggering your lizard brain, try "touching the treadmill," starting with a small, simple step toward your goal that allows you to get started.

- To further help you avoid the resistance to change, frame the entire process as a learning goal. Focus on getting better rather than being good.

Exercises

Something you can do in less than a minute

Look back at positive habits you tried to develop—anything from flossing to playing the piano to exercising regularly. Think about the times you achieved your goal and the times you didn't. What was the difference?

Something you can do in less than 5 minutes

Peer support helps you through the ups and downs of trying to change. Think of people you know who could provide positive, nonjudgmental support as you go through your own guided mastery program. They would be the kinds of people, for example, with whom you would be comfortable sharing ideas in this book. Write down their names.

Level One:
Getting Started

Chapter 10

A Practical Goal and Your First Relationship List

Faith is taking the first step even when you don't see the whole staircase.
—Martin Luther King Jr.

Much of what you'll be doing throughout your guided mastery program is based on asking yourself three questions:

1. What am I trying to accomplish?
2. Who can help me with that goal?
3. How can I contribute to them to deepen our relationship?

It all starts with a simple goal, perhaps exploring a new area of interest or developing your skills at work. Because there's an infinite amount of possible contributing and connecting you can do, having a goal in mind orients your activities and increases your chances of realizing benefits from them. As you work out loud toward a particular goal, you'll be developing skills and a mindset that will help you with almost any goal in the future.

Consider the goals of some of the people in the book so far:

- Jordi wanted to learn more about drones.
- Paul wanted to be more effective at work.
- Barbara wanted to explore other interests.
- Mara wanted to learn more about building communities.
- Joyce wanted to learn more about social media.
- Brandon was exploring the possibility of becoming a photographer.
- I wanted to learn more about collaboration.

Do you see a pattern? The goals were largely about learning and exploring. They were things the individuals genuinely cared about. They were also reasonably specific and something you could make progress toward in twelve weeks. You may have more ambitious goals, like making the world a better place or becoming happier, but such goals are too abstract for a guided mastery program. If your goal is too vague, you'll have trouble identifying a specific set of people who can help you achieve it.

So start by writing down something you would like to accomplish in the next twelve weeks. Don't feel any pressure to get this exactly right. Almost any goal will help orient your activity through part III. In my first Working

Out Loud circle, one person was thinking about becoming a financial advisor and wanted to explore that. Another person was passionate about making people aware of dangerous toxins in products and suggesting alternatives. One started an online fashion consulting business she wanted to grow, and another cared about educational issues. We did the following exercise in about ten minutes and spent a few minutes discussing what we came up with. If you're stuck, you might pick from the most common goals of the people I coach:

- Learn more about something you care about.
- Find a job in a new company or location.
- Get more recognition at your current job.
- Explore possibilities in a new field.
- Find people with the same interests.
- Get better at what you do.

Exercise: Your goal for the next twelve weeks (5 minutes)
Write down your goal for the next twelve weeks now. Keep it to just a sentence or two and less than twenty-five words.

____

____

____

Was that easy enough? When I coach people in person or present to an audience, they have the chance to raise issues or ask questions, such as "I'm too busy," or "Is this the same as personal branding?" Often the real learning comes from the ensuing dialog. So I included the most common issues and questions throughout each chapter in part III. They'll be in *italics*, followed by the response I would give. Here are two questions related to writing down your goal:

Q: What if I don't know my goal?
Abraham Maslow, the psychologist famous for defining our hierarchy of needs, said, "It isn't normal to know what we want. It is a rare and difficult psychological achievement." If your goal isn't clear, consider one of the six common goals listed above. Your goal doesn't necessarily have to be a career goal. It could be anything you care about and want to get better at, even your favorite hobby or raising money for a good cause.

The key for the next twelve weeks isn't so much that you pick the best goal. What's important is that you practice working in a more open, connected way that helps you build relationships. Having that experience and developing the habit of working out loud will better equip you to pursue any goal in the future.

Q: What if I pick the wrong goal?
There is no right or wrong when it comes to goals, but people often do change their goal as they go through the twelve weeks. In my first talk with Barbara, for example, she mentioned she enjoyed giving tax advice, so perhaps exploring that might be her goal. After more thought, she decided to find other people who shared her passion for genealogy and explore possibilities related to that. Then, after two weeks,

she discovered people doing corporate history (in essence, genealogy for companies), and exploring that became her goal.

Hayley's goal was clear when she was working in London and decided to move back to her native Australia. She was heading to a beautiful city on the Coral Sea appropriately named the Gold Coast, and she described her goal this way:

> *To build a purposeful network of people on the Gold Coast that I would enjoy working with, and to find a role in a company that's aligned to my overall purpose and passions.*

That's a good goal. It's clear, something she cares about, and is something she can make meaningful progress toward in twelve weeks.

Your first relationship list

Building your own first list is also easy. Since there's no such thing as *the* definitive network, you don't have to worry about making mistakes. Besides, your list will change over the course of your guided mastery program. Simply by thinking of people who might help you in some way, you'll begin generating more and more ideas. Sometimes you'll know their names ("Sue is the head of my department") and sometimes just their roles ("someone at Company X who does what I do").

Start by thinking of people who already do the thing you're considering as your goal. If you want to explore genealogy or jobs in the Gold Coast, for example, it helps to know people who are already doing things related to genealogy or working in the Gold Coast. Whatever your goal is, here's what you might start looking for:

- People writing about it in blogs, articles, and books
- Online communities related to it
- Businesses you admire that are doing it
- Conferences related to it
- Organizations that support it

Play Internet detective, conducting searches related to your goal. When the people I coach do this for even a few minutes, they quickly start discovering people, companies, and ideas they weren't aware of before. They search, find a lead, follow that with some more searches, and then "Aha! That looks interesting!"

Hayley, for example, used Google to find winners of the Gold Coast Business Excellence Awards, the Chamber of Commerce, the Gold Coast Business Directory, and other existing networks of companies based in the Gold Coast. That's how she found Billabong, SurfStitch, and other firms based there. Then she went to their corporate sites to learn more about their work and about specific people there. She also found people by searching LinkedIn for these organizations. As she was searching, though, she found other things. The Gold Coast is hosting the 2018 Commonwealth Games, something that appealed to Hayley's interest in health and exercise. Looking at the site for the games gave her some ideas. Searching for "Gold Coast Commonwealth Games" led her to a two-minute YouTube interview with the head of marketing and communications for the games. He spoke about a range of work and challenges involved in preparing for such an event. Hayley thought it was interesting, relevant to her goal, and worth learning more about. So she put him on her list.

Exercise: Your first relationship list (15 minutes)

Be the Internet detective. Start searching for people and organizations related to your goal. Try to find ten people. If you find a group or role but can't yet find a name of a specific person, that's OK. Just write down whatever information you have. For now, the most important thing is the searching itself.

1 ____

2 ____

3 ____

4 ____

5 ____

6 ____

7 ____

8 ____

9 ____

10 ____

Q: How do you manage your list?

I remember when, during the course with Keith Ferrazzi, he told us about a complicated spreadsheet he used to manage thousands of contacts. Lots of fields. Color coding. We all wanted it. Surely if we could use the same system as Keith, we could be better at networking, so we pressed him to share his spreadsheet template. By the end of the course, none of us had ever used it, and now it's obvious why that was the case. It turns out that managing contacts is as idiosyncratic as managing tasks, and while some ways are better than others, there is no single best way. What worked for Keith after a few decades of networking was overly complicated for me and for others in the class.

For now, just use this book or get a nice journal to manage your relationship list. In later chapters, I'll suggest a few adjustments and possible improvements to how you manage contacts, but you can go through the entire twelve weeks with just a pen and paper.

Q: What's so special about twelve weeks?

Practice, practice, practice. The only way to develop new habits is through repetition over time. Developing the habit of meditating, for example, requires more than just knowing how to meditate. You have to actually sit down and meditate regularly. How long till something becomes a habit? Studies show that your brain physically changes in three to eight weeks depending on the activity. Through repetition, the activity becomes more automatic and, combined with feedback, you become more proficient. To be conservative, and to account for latency involved when interacting with others in your network, I extended the program to twelve weeks.

Congratulations

If you did both exercises—investing a grand total of about twenty minutes into a goal you care about—you've actually done more than most people. It's not that people are lazy or uncaring. It's just that the changes we want in our careers and our lives can seem so daunting that we don't even know where to begin. I waited till I was in my midforties before I took my first steps.

Now that you've begun, you're ready for another simple and extremely important step.

Key Ideas in this Chapter

- *What are you trying to accomplish?* Goals are typically about learning and exploring. You should pick something that you care about, that is reasonably specific, and that you could make progress toward in twelve weeks.

- *Who can help you with that goal?* Start by thinking of people who are already doing something related to your goal, including people who write about it. Be sure to search for online communities as well as businesses and other organizations related to it.

- Take a moment to congratulate yourself. Just by reading this chapter, thinking about your purpose and people who could help you, you've invested in yourself.

Exercises

Something you can do in less than a minute

Look on Twitter for someone on your list and follow her. The person will receive a notification that you've followed her, and you'll have advanced your relationship in a small way.

Something you can do in less than 5 minutes

Search the Internet for people on your list, looking for blogs or other content they've written. Find at least one person who has a blog that you want to subscribe to and subscribe to it.

Chapter 11

Your First Contributions

Take the first step and your mind will mobilize all its forces to your aid. But the first essential is that you begin.
—Robert Collier

What's something that's free, fun, and feels so good you'll want more of it? Something we all don't get enough of?

You're right. It's appreciation. (That is what you guessed, isn't it?) One of Dale Carnegie's principles is "Give honest and sincere appreciation" and it's one of the first contributions you'll make as you practice leading with generosity. A poignant story from Scott Berkun helped me better understand how everyone values the simple gift of appreciation and why we consistently fail to give it. Scott worked at Microsoft before moving on to become a popular author and speaker. Here's a description of an exchange he had with a colleague as he was about to leave. It contains so many good points I included three entire paragraphs.

On my last day at Microsoft I was invited to do a last lecture. It was a wonderful event and I talked about important things to a friendly crowd. Afterwards, a peer I respected but didn't know walked my way. He thanked me for the work I'd done. I asked why he'd never said anything before. He told me (get this) he thought I already knew. He figured I probably heard that sort of thing all the time. In essence, he didn't want to annoy me with praise. Annoy me with praise! Is there a more absurd phrase in the English language?

It made me think how many times I'd seen or read things that mattered to me and how rare it was I'd offered any praise in return. Books that I loved (or read dozens of times), lectures I enjoyed, good advice I'd received, that I'd never thanked the person for. Or never made an effort to champion their work to others. Dozens of people who said honest things that changed me for the better, or who stuck up for me when others didn't, who never learned the value their words had. I recognized an infinity of actions that made a difference to me that I had not acknowledged in any way and I was poisoned by it. I was less than the man who'd thanked me on my way out of the company. He did something about what mattered to him. He walked straight up, looked me in the eye, and offered his thanks, something, I realized, I didn't know how to do.

These little forgotten things, a short e-mail, a comment on a website, a handshake and a thank you, were not

> *things I'd ever learned. And I realized, in my twisted little attic of a mind, in a hidden dark corner covered in dust, was the belief that offering praise in those contexts was a lessening of my self-opinion. That to compliment was to admit a kind of failure in myself: an association between those kinds of praise and sycophancy. I know now what a fool I've been, for it takes a better man to acknowledge goodness in others than it does to merely be good oneself. Anyone can criticize or accept praise, but initiating a positive exchange is a hallmark of a difference maker.*[1]

I was struck by how Scott saw the value of "little forgotten things" and how they were contributions he simply never learned to make. So let's start by learning how to make these contributions to people on your list.

Exercise: Giving a gift everybody wants (15 minutes)

Today most people have some kind of online presence. Search the Internet for each person on your list, and see what you can find. Look for Twitter accounts, LinkedIn accounts, blogs, or other online content they've produced. If they have Twitter accounts, follow them. In contrast to Facebook and LinkedIn, following someone on Twitter doesn't require the other person to do anything. That's one reason why Twitter is often the simplest and most effective way to take a first step in forming a connection.

If you see a website in a person's Twitter or LinkedIn profile, go to that website and look for content. If you like any of it, let the person know by hitting a Favorite or Like button. If you want to keep receiving updates, look for a Follow button or the ability to subscribe by e-mail. There's no need to worry about what to say or write. You're just touching the treadmill. For now, all you're looking for is an unobtrusive way to move the relationship from *they have no idea who I am* to *they've seen my name.* In the space provided below, write down where online you found each person on your relationship list.

1	______________	______________
2	______________	______________
3	______________	______________
4	______________	______________
5	______________	______________
6	______________	______________
7	______________	______________
8	______________	______________
9	______________	______________
10	______________	______________

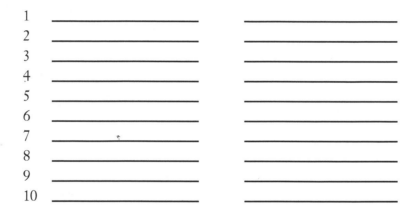

Q: I hate Twitter. I don't get it. Do I have to use it?

I used to hate Twitter too. When I first started using it, I didn't see how it could be valuable. My stream seemed full of trivial oversharing, and so I closed my account. About a year later, though, I discovered *The Twitter Book*, by Sarah Milstein and Tim O'Reilly. Their easy-to-read book showed me how and why I could get value from Twitter. You certainly don't have to use it, but as part of working out loud,

Twitter is the simplest way to find and listen to people you would never reach otherwise. By doing the exercises, you'll learn what to post. For now, just use it to find people on your list and follow them.

Your full range of contributions

The like or follow you offered in that exercise might seem trivial, but it was just a first simple step. During the rest of your guided mastery program, you'll learn about making more significant contributions, ones that take more effort but have more value both to you and the people in your network. You'll practice generosity with more people in a wider variety of contexts, and you'll discover other gifts you have to offer. Even with simple contributions, though, there is a broad spectrum of possibilities. Thinking through them will help expand your very notion of "contribution."

Besides the like and follow in the exercise, can you think of other simple gifts you might offer both in person and online? Here's a list of ten gifts anyone can offer. See if you can come up with at least one more.

1 Read what someone wrote.
2 Give someone your full attention when she is speaking.
3 Congratulate someone on a new job or other milestone.
4 Recognize someone by pointing out his work or positive qualities.
5 Appreciate someone with a public thank-you.
6 Offer your encouragement.

7 Offer your support.
8 Ask questions, allowing others to share their expertise.
9 Share entertainment you've enjoyed.
10 Share resources—books, presentations, articles—that you've found useful.

Exercise: So much to offer! (10 minutes)

Now, for everyone on your relationship list, ask yourself, "What do I have to offer that can further develop the relationship?" Use the list above as a guide. For example, I admire the work of Austin Kleon, author of *Steal Like an Artist* and *Show Your Work*, and I've already followed him on Twitter. What are other contributions I might make? Remember Scott Berkun's "annoy me with praise." Since I like Austin's work, items four, five, eight, and ten from the list seem like good, simple gifts to offer. I could recognize his work, thank him, ask a question about his writing, and share why I liked his books. Doing any of that publicly is something even a best-selling author will find helpful and will appreciate. It's also a nice thing to do.

You don't have to actually give the gifts right now. Just go through each person on your relationship list, identify at least one extra contribution for him or her, and write that contribution next to the person's name.

1 ____________________ ____________________
2 ____________________ ____________________

3	________________	________________
4	________________	________________
5	________________	________________
6	________________	________________
7	________________	________________
8	________________	________________
9	________________	________________
10	________________	________________

Q: Is that it? How will this help me?

While offering these specific gifts to these people won't change your luck right away, taking this first step is critical to developing new habits and a new mindset. The quote at the top of the chapter from Robert Collier, an American author on practical psychology and becoming your best, among other topics, captured the power of such initial efforts: "Take the first step and your mind will mobilize all its forces to your aid." It's like buying a pair of red shoes or considering a new kind of car and suddenly seeing more of them everywhere. By paying attention to something, your mind becomes more attuned to it.

I see this with the people I coach. As they start experiencing networking as something based on contributions instead of transactions, they tend to have a similar reaction: "I never thought of it that way before." They start to see more possible contributions everywhere, including things they had never even considered framing as a contribution.

Week after week, they get better and more creative. They add more people and more contributions and tap into new possibilities they didn't see earlier. They're ready for more.

Key Ideas in this Chapter

- One of Dale Carnegie's principles is "Give honest and sincere appreciation," and it's one of the first contributions you'll make as you practice leading with generosity.

- A small gesture of appreciation is recognizing the other person's work online. It could be as simple as following the person on Twitter or subscribing to her blog.

- If you think people you admire may not value your recognition, remember Scott Berkun's story about the value of "the little forgotten things." A*nnoy me with praise!*

- Even with simple contributions, there is a broad spectrum of possibilities. During the rest of your guided mastery program, you'll learn about more significant contributions that take more effort but have more value both to you and the people in your network.

Exercises

Something you can do in less than a minute

Go to your list from the last exercise in this chapter, pick the easiest contribution there, and make it right now. Every action like this reinforces your new positive habit of asking, "What do I have to offer that can further develop the relationship?"

As an example, here's a small contribution I made to Austin Kleon, a token of my appreciation for his work.

Here's a newsletter I love. It's a weekly dose of serendipity with goldilocks portions of creativity, wit & wisdom austinkleon.com/newsletter/

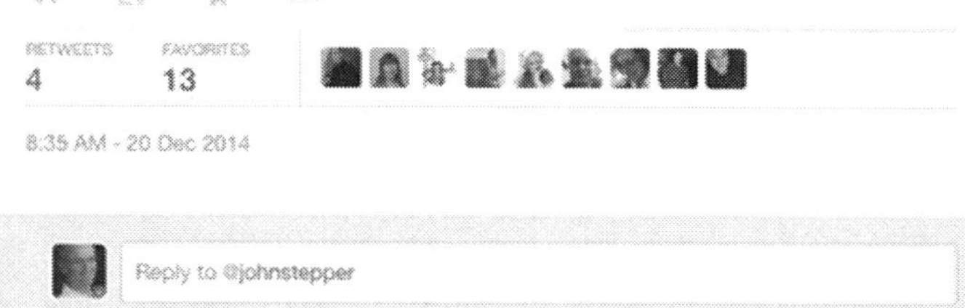

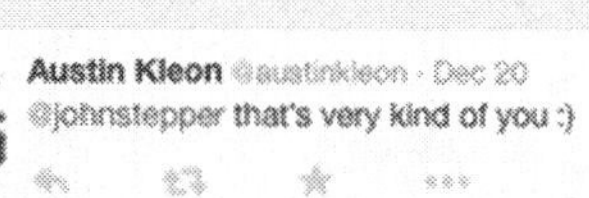

Something you can do in less than 5 minutes

Look at your list, and find a contribution that's more than a like or follow. Perhaps someone on your list wrote something—a blog, an article, a book—that you liked or found interesting or useful. Let the person know by posting a comment or by mentioning him on Twitter and linking to the content.

Here's an example. I just referred to Scott Berkun's post in this chapter. But did I comment on his post? No. Did I share his post with my network and describe why I liked it? No. So, to demonstrate how easy it is, I just did both those things in less than five minutes. Scott, whom I don't know, replied later that same day.

The tweet was easy to write and was quickly retweeted by a friend.

Love this by @berkun on showing appreciation, etc: "These little forgotten things..were not things I'd ever learned." scottberkun.com/essays/49-how-...

The comment took longer to write, perhaps four minutes, but felt more personal, so the extra time was worth it to me.

 JOHN STEPPER | JUNE 2, 2014 #

I loved this post. I first read it last month in "Mindfire" and then came back to it here. Since then, I've retold your story and used "Annoy me with praise!" to show how rarely we offer the universal gifts of appreciation and recognition. I hope to use the story in a book I'm writing called "Working Out Loud."

One particular line struck me. "These little forgotten things....were not things I'd ever learned." I think the general lack of appreciation we experience isn't due to some flaw in our make-up or some sinister reasoning but simply ignorance: most people don't know how to do it. And even those who do tend not to have a method or practice for doing it consistently.

Those are easier problems to solve. And that gives me hope.

I know you wrote this 6 years ago, but I'll take the risk of annoying you with praise and say thanks again for a great post. :-)

SCOTT | JUNE 2, 2014 #

Thanks John. As corny as it sounds I reread this essay now and then as I I know I forget to take its advice. Many of these philosophical essays were/are written to help me remind myself of things I forget.

Chapter 12

Working Your Lists

Repetition of the same thought or physical action develops into a habit which, repeated frequently enough, becomes an automatic reflex.

—Norman Vincent Peale

Before we take the next small step, it's time to talk about time. One of the biggest barriers to developing yourself and your career—and one of the themes of modern life—is being busy. People simply don't have the time to do the things they know would be good for them, whether that's exercising or eating right or, ahem, doing the exercises in this book.

I found a cure for this problem in a book called *The Richest Man in Babylon.* When a smart, successful person recommended this book to me, I was expecting rich historical fiction or perhaps some stimulating anthropology. Instead, it was a seventy-one-page, poorly typeset pamphlet published in 1926 about "thrift and financial success, using parables set in Babylon to make each of [the author's] points."[1] The author was George Clason, owner of a map company in Colorado, and banks and insurance companies distributed the pamphlet to help teach customers how to manage their money. Despite its humble appearance and purpose, this simple guide about managing money held valuable lessons for managing other important resources, including time.

The richest man in Babylon's first and most important lesson was to set aside 10 percent of your money before spending anything. "A part of all you earn is yours to keep. It should not be less than a tenth no matter how little you earn…Pay yourself first."[2] You can use the same approach with time. Before you schedule your first meeting or take on another responsibility, schedule time to invest in yourself. Start with as little as fifteen minutes a day or an hour a week. You'll use that time to do research related to your goal and develop relationships in your network or to do the exercises in the book and meet with your Working Out Loud circle.

Exercise: Pay yourself first (5 minutes)

To pay yourself first, take a look at your calendar now, and make appointments with yourself over the next week for doing the activities relating to your goal and working out loud toward that goal. Write down the slots you picked.

____

____

____

Q: I want to invest in myself, but I really don't have time.
Though we all have different jobs and different schedules, almost no one feels he has extra time. After all, your time is already accounted for, so when you choose to do something new, you have to make a trade of some kind. For example, whenever you say yes to a meeting or a task, you're saying no to something else that could be much more valuable. Ask yourself, "What's the something else?"

Even in 1926, George Clason recognized that "What each of us calls our 'necessary expenses' will always grow to equal our incomes unless we protest to the contrary."[3] Since your time is most likely fully allocated, you probably won't find *spare* time. But you can identify activities you'll start saying no to so you can invest in things more important to you in the long term.

The richest man in Babylon also advised to "guard thy treasures from loss" and to avoid wasteful ventures. Average Americans may consider themselves busy, but they also spend more than 34 hours a week watching TV.[4] Whether or not you consider that a good investment, the point is that you can't make extra time. All you can do is make conscious decisions on how you spend the time you have. The exercise is aimed at helping you exchange low-value activities for a bit more time investing in yourself.

Q: There's no way I can find time in my schedule. Now what?
I completely understand. If you feel like you already have a full week, finding an hour can be daunting. Here are a few things you might do:

- Check that your goal is something you care about. The more you care about it, the more motivated you'll be to find time to work on it.
- If one hour a week is too much, try half an hour. If that's too much, try two fifteen-minute increments. Just be sure to schedule them.
- If you're still struggling, keep a time journal for a week. Track how you're spending time, even in fifteen-minute increments. Review it at the end of the week, and ask what the richest man in Babylon might say. Did you pay yourself first? Did you invest your time wisely? I did this exercise myself when I thought I didn't have enough time to work on the book. After a few days, it became clear I was spending more time on my phone—checking Facebook and meandering on the Internet—than I had thought. I cut back on that and invested that time in writing.

Working the lists

As you schedule time and pay yourself first, one of the things you'll do regularly is consider each person on your relationship list and practice asking "What do I have to offer that can further develop the relationship?" Now you're ready to create another list: your contribution list. That's where you'll list all the things you have to offer and ask a different question: "For whom might this be a contribution?"

To show you how this works, let's use the contribution list from the last chapter. As you reach advanced levels of working out loud, you'll add more original and valuable contributions to this list. For now, though, this is more than enough for getting started. Here's the contribution list from the last chapter:

1. Read what someone wrote.
2. Give someone your full attention when she is speaking.
3. Congratulate someone on a new job or other milestone.
4. Recognize someone by pointing out his work or positive qualities.
5. Appreciate someone with a public thank-you.
6. Offer your encouragement.
7. Offer your support.
8. Ask questions, allowing others to share their expertise.
9. Share entertainment you've enjoyed.
10. Share resources—books, presentations, articles—that you've found useful.

Let's practice with the last one on the list. Suppose you've just finished *Lean In*, by Sheryl Sandberg, and you felt, as I did, that it was well written and full of practical advice. Great. Now ask, "For whom might this be a contribution?" Whenever you've read or watched or done something useful, that's an asset, a possible contribution. Perhaps there are women in your network who might benefit from reading it, or maybe recent graduates or others who could use career help. Then you would go through your relationship list and, next to all the people who might benefit from that contribution, decide on the best way to offer it.

Once you have an asset and start thinking of people who would benefit from you sharing it, other names often come to mind for your relationship list. There's an interplay between the two lists. As you go through relationships, you think of more possible contributions. As you go through contributions, you think of more relationships you would like to develop.

Exercise: A gift for that special someone (20 minutes)
Think of a particular resource—book, TED talk, article—that you've found useful, and list it here:

____

Practice asking yourself "For whom might this be a contribution?" Try to list five people. (10 minutes)

1. ____________________________________
2. ____________________________________
3. ____________________________________
4. ____________________________________
5. ____________________________________

Now try the exact opposite exercise. Pick one of these people, and think of five possible contributions for him or her using your contributions list as a guide. (10 minutes)

Person on your list: __________________________

1. ____________________
2. ____________________
3. ____________________
4. ____________________
5. ____________________

Q: What if I'm having trouble finding people?
Your main objective in creating your relationship list is to find people related to your goal. If you're considering becoming a financial advisor, find financial advisors. Considering moving to the Gold Coast, Australia? Start looking at people and companies who are already there. Broaden your search to go beyond people who have already achieved your goal to people who write, speak, or provide services related to your goal. Once you find one person, try to see who that person is connected to. Play Internet detective, and keep following the trail of connections.

Q: I couldn't think of many contributions. What's wrong?
You're just getting started, so this is natural. Know that a simple thank-you or other sign of genuine appreciation can be among the most powerful gifts you have. You'll learn about more advanced contributions in the rest of part III.

Q: It feels fake.
If it feels fake or inauthentic, stop. Only offer genuine gifts. If you didn't love *Lean In*, for example, don't say you did. Even more importantly, if you loved something and shared it,

don't worry about a response. It's the expectation of getting something in return that can spoil a gift. Offering contributions should make you feel good. If you don't have positive feelings as you work your lists, reconsider the gifts you're offering and whether you're truly delivering them without any strings attached.

Are you ready for the next level?

Was that difficult for you? Were you uncertain whether you were doing it the right way? If so, that's a typical part of the learning process. You're simply doing something you're not used to doing. Some people get through these exercises in two weeks while others take two months. It's not a competition, and there's no test at the end. We're all just getting better at answering the questions "What do I have to offer that can further develop the relationship?" and "For whom might this be a contribution?"

By repeatedly working the lists over time, you'll gradually find that thinking in terms of relationships and contributions comes more naturally. Members of Working Out Loud circles say that talking through the exercises seems to make it easier. As they go through their relationship lists with other people, they come up with more names. As they talk through possible contributions, they come up with more things to offer. They're on their way to developing a new set of habits and are ready to strengthen those habits.

Key Ideas in this Chapter

- One of the biggest barriers to developing yourself and your career is being busy. To reallocate your time, consider that every time you say yes to something, you're saying no to something else.

- Think of time as a valuable resource, and remember to invest in yourself. Remember to *pay yourself first.*

- You want to develop the habit of regularly reviewing your relationship list and asking, "What do I have to offer that can further develop the relationship?"

- You also want to review your contribution list and, for each item, ask, "For whom might this be a contribution?"

- By repeatedly working your lists, thinking in terms of relationships and contributions will come more naturally over time.

Exercises

Something you can do in less than a minute

Pick someone on your list and offer thanks on Twitter for something the person has done. One friend called this exercise "cheesy," but I feel it's only cheesy if you don't mean it. A genuine public thank-you is a wonderful gift. Give one now, and update your relationship list with the date and gift next to that person's name.

Something you can do in less than 5 minutes

If you're like me, you're somewhat haunted by all the unsent thank-you cards in your life. So here's a chance to make amends. Pick someone on your list, and offer a private thank-you via e-mail. Just two or three sentences that say you've been thinking of the person and wanted to say thank you for something he or she did or said.

Everyone would love to get such a note. So send one now, and update your relationship list with the date and your gift next to that person's name.

Chapter 13

Making It a Habit

Habits shape our lives far more than we realize—
they are so strong, in fact, that they cause our brains
to cling to them at the exclusion of all else, including common sense.
—Charles Duhigg, *The Power of Habit*

In the book *Strangers to Ourselves,* Timothy Wilson writes that while our brains can take in eleven million pieces of information at any given moment, we're only consciously aware of forty. Only forty! It's a dramatic statistic that shows just how precious little attention we have and why change is so hard. Acquiring a new skill or behavior requires that we focus our precious attention over a period of time, and, since attention is scarce, we have a natural aversion to expending it. As the neurologist Daniel Kahneman writes, "Laziness is built deep into our nature."[1]

Habits are one way of helping us deal with the complexity of life and all the information in it. With the repetition of an act, effort decreases over time as the brain physically changes. The activity becomes easier, more automatic. The more we do it, the less we have to think about it. For most people reading this book, even if you've made a conscious decision to work out loud, it's only when you've turned that choice into a habit that your actions will consistently be in line with your intentions. We see this regularly in our Working Out Loud circles. The meetings start with a review of the work everyone did the previous week—the people they reached out to, the contributions they made. By reviewing what worked and what didn't work, people in the circle get a chance to offer suggestions and help each other make adjustments.

Even in the most committed circles, though, people will have weeks when they struggle to make any progress. If that happens, they needn't feel bad. It's a natural part of their learning process, of getting better. So before moving on to more advanced techniques, this chapter will help you develop new habits by giving you a framework for making steady, consistent progress.

How to make a habit of anything

When it comes to making some positive change in your life, much of the wisdom and research I discovered in a decade of reading self-help books was distilled into a simple, practical list in *Coach Yourself* by Anthony Grant and Jane Greene. The ten items in their list form a checklist for changing anything in your life:

1. Take small steps toward your goals.
2. Set some realistic, achievable goals.

3. Structure your life to help you attain your goals.
4. Chart your progress.
5. Look at the areas where you're successful.
6. Reward yourself for your successes.
7. Focus on your achievements.
8. Allow yourself to fail without turning it into a catastrophe.
9. Enlist the support of friends.
10. Picture the way you'd like life to be.[2]

Looking back, whenever I failed to do something that took a lot of effort, it was because I missed one or more elements on this list. When I initially failed to make headway on the book, for example, it was because I didn't chart my progress and hadn't organized any peer support. When I kept saying I was going to do yoga regularly but failed, it was because I tried to do too much too soon and my defense mechanisms found ways to avoid it. Changing my eating habits took the longest. I didn't "structure my life to help me attain my goal." Pro tip: if you want to eat fewer snacks or drink less wine, don't keep so much of it in the house.

Before going into ways to make working out loud a habit, try this short assessment and apply the checklist to your own attempts at working out loud so far.

Exercise: The "change anything" checklist (5 minutes)

Look again at each of the ten items in the above checklist and consider how they apply to you and your own approach. Circle the ones you think deserve the most attention. The rest of this chapter will describe ways to help you with each item.

Take small steps toward realistic, achievable goals

A common goal-related problem I see in our Working Out Loud circles is when people choose something they *think* they should care about but don't. For example, it makes intellectual sense to want more recognition at work. But if you don't like your job or the people you work with, it's hard to summon the energy you'll need to pay attention and work out loud toward that goal. When I worked with Barbara, we spoke about possible goals related to her current job or possibly pursuing other careers in finance. But those ideas didn't feel right or inspiring. So she chose a simpler goal of simply "seeing what else is out there" related to her genealogy hobby. For Barbara, exploring people and possibilities related to something she was passionate about was a much better way to orient her working out loud activities. It made it much more attractive for her brain to devote attention to it.

Lesson: If you're not inspired by your goal, pick one that relates to something you're genuinely interested in.

Another common problem related to goals is taking on too much too soon. Particularly ambitious people sometimes select multiple goals or try to quickly establish large networks full of important people. That might work for them.

But if it's not working for you, break your goals down into smaller chunks, and set smaller, more readily achievable targets each week. Disappointments early on make it more difficult to maintain the sustained effort you'll need to develop new habits.

Lesson: If you're not making steady, regular progress toward your goal, consider choosing a simpler goal or taking smaller interim steps toward your goal. In developing new habits, regular practice and feedback is more important than being ambitious.

Structure your life to help you attain your goals

This one item on the checklist is perhaps the most important. "Structure your life" might sound daunting, but it just means fashioning an environment that makes it easier for you to do what you need to do. In *The Power of Habit*, Charles Duhigg quotes someone who has developed training specifically for reversing unwanted habits: "Once you're aware of how your habit works, once you recognize the cues and rewards, you're halfway to changing it...It seems like it should be more complex. The truth is, the brain can be reprogrammed. You just have to be deliberate about it."

How might that relate to working out loud? Here are four cues you can create to help you:

Schedule the time to do it. Researching people on your list. Interacting with them online. Drafting personalized notes or other content. Meeting with your Working Out Loud circle. When you schedule the times you'll practice these activities, you don't have to think about when to fit them in or juggle your task lists. The less you have to think about it, the less attention you'll have to spend and the easier it will be to do it consistently.

Create rituals. Your physical environment can also serve as a set of cues to put you in the right frame of mind for working out loud. Cues might include sitting in your special writing chair with a special notebook and pen dedicated to your new habit or sitting with your laptop and a cup of mint tea in your favorite cafe. Over time, those cues will tell you "Now is the time to work out loud," and you'll expend less mental energy getting started.

Set up visual cues. These can be simple physical reminders, like a note taped to your computer. For example, if you asked yourself, "What's the contribution?" every time you sent an e-mail, that would be dozens of opportunities to practice every day. Over time, you would be framing things as contributions without even thinking about it. That alone would be a powerful habit.

Voice the intention. This is something we do in our Working Out Loud circles at the end of each meeting: we tell each other what we plan to do in the coming week. To further reinforce our intent, we share it via e-mail after the meeting. Finally, if you're really having trouble accomplishing some task, like sending a note to someone on your list, specify the time and place you'll do it.

Lesson: Create cues and structures so at certain times and places you're automatically in the mode of working out loud. This reduces the cognitive burden related to developing a new habit and makes it easier for you to practice.

Make your progress visible

While I was working on this book, my friends would often ask, "How's the book coming along?" I would say it was going well, and they would offer encouragement. But when my wife asked me the same question, the conversation took a different turn. She was the one, after all, who saw me brooding in front of my laptop for countless hours. When I told her that the book was going well, she had a few more questions.

When will it be done?
I don't know. I really don't have enough time.

How much more time do you need?
I don't know.

How nuch time have you spent on it so far?
I don't know.

How nuch did you work on it last week? Or yesterday even?
I don't know.

A long, awkward silence ensued. Inside my head were two other questions: "Did Hemingway's wife ask him these questions?" More importantly: "Am I just kidding myself?"

Instead of trying to defend my lack of a meaningful publishing plan, I made an adjustment that morning that enabled me to publish the book: I made a chart. It was a simple calendar with a space for every day of the month. In each space, I would write down how many hours a day I worked on the book. Instead of the story I was telling myself—*I'm writing a book!*—the data on the chart showed I wasn't working on it nearly enough. That was the push I needed to set up a regular writing schedule.

Lesson: Visible feedback on the effort you're expending will make you aware of adjustments you need to make.

Reflect, learn, and encourage yourself

Items 5 through 8 on the checklist, 40 percent of the list, relate to using positive reinforcement to encourage and motivate you:

- Look at the areas where you're successful.
- Reward yourself for your successes.
- Focus on your achievements.
- Allow yourself to fail without turning it into a catastrophe.

That's because positive reinforcement is more effective by far than any other method. Yet many of us were raised in an era where "spare the rod, spoil the child" was considered good parenting advice. Too often, our attempts at self-motivation are harsh, overly critical, and unforgiving.

Animal trainers have long known better. It's why they can reliably reproduce extraordinary behaviors in animals while we humans resort to yelling, threats, and force. Karen Pryor is a behavioral biologist, a pioneering dolphin trainer, and an authority on applied operant conditioning—the art and science of changing behavior. In *Don't Shoot the Dog*, she describes her behavioral methods and how they apply even beyond animal training:

> *I began to notice some applications of the system creeping into my daily life. For example, I stopped yelling at my kids, because I was noticing that yelling didn't work. Watching for behavior I liked, and reinforcing it when it occurred, worked a lot better and kept the peace, too.*[3]

One of Karen Pryor's fellow dolphin researchers quipped, "Nobody should be allowed to have a baby until they have first been required to train a chicken." When it comes to using positive reinforcement to motivate ourselves to develop new habits, chicken training would indeed be useful experience.

> *Lesson: Actively look for successes and the reasons behind them and reinforce them with self-praise and other rewards. When you fail, avoid self-criticism, and simply embrace that failure is a natural part of the learning process. Then commit to applying that learning in your next effort.*

Enlist the support of friends

In chapter 5, we saw that all sorts of social behaviors flow through social networks. If your friends are overweight, you're more likely to be overweight. If your spouse is in a bad mood, you're more likely to be in a bad mood. The more intimate the bond, the more readily behaviors of one person will affect another.

Peer support groups have formed around topics as diverse as abstinence, changing eating habits, and public speaking. That's because they're effective, and that's why we formed Working Out Loud circles. Whether the circle winds up being you and your spouse or a small group of friends, colleagues, or even strangers, the shared accountability and support can make the process of change significantly easier.

Lesson: Change can be a lot easier when you're going through it with someone else. Try to find at least one other person who wants to work out loud like you do. Form a Working Out Loud circle if you can, since the added structure of the circle will further increase your chances of success. There's a section on circles at the end of the book.

Picture the way you would like life to be

Almost any book on change will talk about the value of envisioning the future. There are many exercises related to this, from describing your ideal day to cutting out pictures that represent your desired future life to writing your own eulogy. I've found one particular exercise so useful that it's the sole topic of chapter 17.

Exercise: Voice the intention (15 minutes)

Now look one more time at each of the ten items in the above checklist and the ones you circled as needing the most attention. Take this opportunity to *voice the intention* and write down which adjustments you'll make.

Each item on the "change anything" checklist will make it easier for you to work out loud, making a habit of thinking in terms of relationships and contributions. Each time you practice will help reinforce that habit and enable you to move on to the next level, *connecting*.

Key Ideas in this Chapter

- It takes effort to develop new habits but little effort to sustain them. *Laziness is built deep into our nature.*

- A checklist for changing anything in your life:

1. Take small steps toward your goals.
2. Set some realistic, achievable goals.
3. Structure your life to help you attain your goals.
4. Chart your progress.
5. Look at the areas where you're successful.
6. Reward yourself for your successes.
7. Focus on your achievements.
8. Allow yourself to fail without turning it into a catastrophe.
9. Enlist the support of friends.
10. Picture the way you'd like life to be.

Exercises

Something you can do in less than a minute
Look at your calendar for the next week, and schedule the times you'll work on working out loud. Try and invest at least fifteen minutes a day or perhaps an hour a week. Any time is better than none.

Something you can do in less than 5 minutes
Create a physical chart of your progress. It could be as simple as my own chart, a plain sheet of paper I taped to the wall that has a space for every day of the month. Use your chart to track the time you're investing in yourself and in your new habit of working out loud.

Level Two:
Connecting

Chapter 14

Deepening Relationships through Contribution

The fact that I'm me and no one else is one of my greatest assets.
—Haruki Murakami, *What I Talk About When I Talk About Running*

Do you remember Mara, the woman from New Zealand in chapter 1? She discovered other people and other projects and wound up creating a new kind of job at her firm. A few years later, she had a different purpose: she wanted to go home. Mara had spent a large part of her life in New Zealand, and much of her family was still there. She had come to London for work and enjoyed it there, but she missed the natural beauty of New Zealand and thought the schools there would be better for her children. The problem was finding a job.

"Do you think my firm would relocate me?" she asked me.

Maybe. But her firm had only a few dozen employees in New Zealand whereas there were 4.5 million people in the country. Surely Mara could increase her odds by looking outside her firm too. So I began helping her with her new goal. Unlike the last time, she wasn't trying to escape a job she didn't like. She was simply exploring possibilities, trying to increase the chances of finding meaningful and fulfilling work. In effect, she was buying career insurance. What if her firm wouldn't relocate her? What if the management in New Zealand didn't appreciate what she did? Bad answers to those questions could throw Mara's life into turmoil. Rather than just hope for the best, she was going to create other options just in case. That gave her more control and less anxiety.

Starting to make more significant contributions

Mara did all the things you did in the Getting Started section. She wrote down her purpose and drew up a relationship list. She played Internet detective and started following people and liking things.

"Now what?" she asked me.

What happened next is an example of what can happen to you, and it provides the motivation for the exercises in this chapter. One of the people on Mara's list was the CEO of a large company in New Zealand. Mara liked what the company did and saw the CEO was active on Twitter, so she followed him. Then she read his posts and occasionally retweeted some of them or praised them. That led to a simple "thank you" in reply.

None of these individual actions took much effort or involved much risk, but Mara had gone from *he doesn't know I exist* to *we've interacted.* Then it got more interesting. In one particular tweet, the CEO posted a complaint about a social platform his firm was using. This was something Mara had ideas and opinions about, so she replied, and he asked her to send him an e-mail. Aha! Now this would be a different kind of contribution. It would take more thought and more time to write, but it could be more valuable to the CEO and deepen their relationship. She carefully crafted her e-mail, long enough to contain some good ideas but short enough that he would still read it. He replied. Those e-mails led to a phone call via Skype and then another call. The phone calls gave Mara a better understanding of the problems the CEO had and other contributions she could make. Now she had moved the relationship from *we've interacted* to *we're collaborating.*

There are several lessons we can draw from Mara's approach, and these lessons resulted in three simple exercises.

Exercise: Intimacy levels (3 minutes)

It helps to be conscious that not all relationships in your network are the same. The most obvious way they differ is the depth of the connection. Here, as a guide, is an intimacy scale from zero to five:

0—The person doesn't know you exist.
1—You're connected in some way.
2—You've had one or more interactions.

3—You've collaborated.
4—You regularly call on each other.
5—You're a trusted advisor.

You're not trying to go from zero to five in one attempt, and you don't need to get to level five with everyone. You're simply trying, over time, to deepen some of your relationships. For this quick exercise, go through your relationship list, and write down your intimacy level for each person on the list.

Q: Where should I write this down?
Now that you're becoming a connector, you'll need a better system to track relationships than scribbling in this book. The people I've coached started with a simple list on paper or on a computer, and some continue that way. Most people, including Mara, eventually switched to using a spreadsheet, Evernote, or another simple application that they can access on their phone or tablet. Simplicity and convenience are the most important attributes of any system you choose. I still keep my list on a piece of paper that I carry with me and rewrite each week. Because my list is so accessible, I refer to it more often, and I'm more mindful of the people on it.

A step toward a more systematic approach

After Mara worked her relationship list for two weeks, she noticed that she cared about some relationships more than others. More precisely, she wanted to invest more in certain relationships. After following people and their activity for a few weeks, she found a few people whose work she was particularly interested in. Also, some were more active on social media, which made it easier. So instead of going through everyone on her relationship list every week and thinking of a possible contribution, we used a simple system to help her focus.

For each person, we kept track of three additional things:

1. The last contribution she made.
2. The date she made it.
3. The date she'd like to make another one.

Here are some examples:

Relationship: CEO
Last contribution: retweeted something he posted
Date of last contribution: June 4
Date of next contribution: June 6

Relationship: Recruiter
Last contribution: Liked his post on LinkedIn
Date of last contribution: June 4
Date of next contribution: July 18

Relationship: Social Media Person at a New Zealand Bank
Last contribution: none yet
Date of last contribution: not yet
Date of next contribution: August 15

This simple adjustment helped make her networking efforts more systematic. For the CEO, she was willing to spend more time and effort in the relationship. So she would pay more attention to his online activity and be sure to make some kind of contribution every few days or so. For a recruiter she just discovered, she wasn't sure how much she wanted to invest in the relationship, so she set a reminder to make some kind of contribution within six weeks or so. In the third example, she didn't yet know what the contribution might be and hadn't learned much about the person yet, so she entered a date even further out. Something might happen in the interim to make Mara more interested in these relationships, and now she had a system that made it easier to keep track and not lose touch entirely with people in her network.

Exercise: From ad hoc to systematic (10 minutes)
Go through your own relationship list, and add the three new bits of information for each person.

Q: It seems complicated. Is this really necessary?
It's not necessary, but it is extremely useful. Even people who say they know networking is important will routinely tell me, "I know I should follow up, but I don't." Maintaining a relationship list will solve that problem. Start with a simple list you can access on your phone or computer. Then schedule a time once a week to look at it and update it. It might take ten minutes per week. The practice of reviewing that list will help you to be mindful of the relationships you want

to invest in and will relieve you of the need to keep all your intended follow-ups in your head.

Additional ways to make contributions

The contributions you've been making so far have been simple and universal. That's a great way to start. Now you want to take a step toward making gifts that are more meaningful to both you and the recipients.

When Mara replied to the CEO and then wrote an e-mail specifically for him, she was offering contributions that took more time and effort but also had more potential value. As she practiced going through her relationship list, she became more mindful that the things she was doing and learning were all possible contributions for people in her growing network. For each person on her relationship list, she started to keep track of multiple contributions she might make in the future. Here are ten examples of more significant contributions you can consider making:

1. Answer questions others have asked.
2. Offer a comment that builds on someone's work.
3. Share your ideas.
4. Share something you've learned.
5. Share your work experiences, especially mistakes.
6. Share your life experiences.
7. Share your challenges.
8. Offer introductions to people you know.
9. Offer your skills.
10. Offer your time.

While our lists of possible contributions and possible relationships continue to grow, keep in mind that all you're really doing is answering two basic questions: *What's the contribution?* and *Who's it for?* The first question reminds you to lead with generosity in deepening a specific relationship. The second question reminds you that a single contribution can be useful to more than one person in your network. The two lists, one for relationships and one for contributions, are there as helpful reminders of how to answer those two questions. Here are some examples from Mara:

Answer questions others have asked. Mara actively looked for opportunities to be helpful, so when the CEO posted an issue on Twitter, she replied.

Offer a comment that builds on someone's work. Share your ideas. Mara was one of two hundred thousand members of the Kiwi Expat Association (for New Zealanders who lived abroad). She liked the group and saw, based on examples from other companies, how they could engage their members even more. So she shared those ideas with the online community.

Share your work experiences, especially mistakes. On Mara's relationship list, for example, were several people who worked in New Zealand banks and had jobs related to Mara's. Since Mara worked in a bank, she sent personalized e-mails offering to share her experiences.

The more she practiced answering the two basic questions—"What's the contribution?" and "Who's it for?"—the more she saw that she already possessed a wide range of gifts she could offer. Think of the Murakami quote at the beginning of this chapter: "The fact that I'm me and no one else is one of my greatest assets." Here are ten facts about Mara that could be the basis of yet more contributions:

- She is raising two children.
- She lived in London.
- She spends time on a small island in Croatia.
- She is a woman.
- She works in a bank.
- She has learned a lot about social media.
- She has lived in different countries.
- She made some career choices she wouldn't make again.
- She knows about rugby.
- She has given talks at conferences.

Each of these as well as a hundred other things about Mara could be gifts for someone if framed as a contribution. Mara's knowledge and experiences might be valuable to people in other banks, to other mothers, to anyone thinking of moving to a new country, to anyone traveling to Croatia or New Zealand, to anyone interested in social media, and to women making career choices. It turns out that the biggest limits to what we have to offer are those we place on ourselves. In becoming a connector, Mara made the shift from offering universal gifts to making contributions that were personal and specific to her. That increased their value both to Mara and to potential recipients.

Exercise: So much to give! (20 minutes)

Here's a simple creative exercise. It might be easier to do with a friend or in a Working Out Loud circle since other people more readily see things about you that you've long taken for granted.

Look at the ten facts about Mara above and write down your own list of facts. Try to get to fifty facts. More is better. When I first did this exercise, I struggled. I felt the things on my list had to be grand accomplishments, not trivial facts. Now I know that any part of my experience—had knee surgery, became a vegetarian, had a mother with diabetes, went to Regis High School—might be interesting to *someone* else if I frame it as a contribution. Not everyone would appreciate every gift, of course, but someone would.

For this exercise, don't worry about who the gift is for. Free yourself, and write down at least fifty facts about you.

Q: I only got to twelve facts.

That's OK. Simply doing the exercise and thinking about what you have to offer is a positive step. If you're struggling to think more broadly about yourself, try doing the exercise for a friend. Examining someone else's life tends to be more comfortable. Then, after you've written fifty facts about a friend, try the exercise again for yourself. For extra credit, contact your friend and tell her you've written fifty things about her that would be contributions for other people. That in itself would make a lovely gift.

Q: I understand, but I'm still not sure what to say.
Focus on simple gifts and how you offer them. Presentation matters. The carefully wrapped present with the handwritten card. The book with a thoughtful inscription. Even a simple postcard or photo that says "I was thinking of you." The value of a gift often has more to do with how it is offered than the worth of the thing itself.

The rules of etiquette and gift giving can seem quite complex, further complicated by technology. Now it's not just what you say and how you say it but which technology you use to say it with. In the next chapter, we'll go through some simple principles and examples that can serve as useful guides for any situation.

Key Ideas in this Chapter

- Some relationships in your network will be more intimate and meaningful than others.
- Keeping track of a few things for each person—your last contribution, the date of that contribution, and the date for the next one—can turn your relationship-building efforts from ad hoc to systematic.
- As you look to help people in your network, you'll keep asking yourself two basic questions: "What's the contribution?" and "Who's it for?"
- The biggest limits to what we have to offer are those we place on ourselves. Remember, when you offer things that are personal and specific to you, they're more meaningful and valuable.

Exercises

Something you can do in less than a minute

In chapter 12, one of the exercises was to think of the last book, article, or TED talk you've really enjoyed and for whom that might be a contribution. Scan your list now, and find one person who might also appreciate it and with whom you're comfortable sending a message. Then send a link via any platform you like—e-mail, text, Twitter, Facebook, or LinkedIn—along with a personal comment like "I loved this, and it made me think of you." A simple message like this can make someone's day and bring you closer.

Something you can do in less than 5 minutes

We all have people in our relationship list that we've wanted to see but have lost touch with. The more time passes, the more we feel bad about it and the tougher it seems to be to do something about it. You can fix that now in less than five minutes. Pick one person on your list that you've been meaning to reach out to and ask him or her to lunch. Make it personal: "I think of you often, and I miss our conversations. Would you like to have lunch together?" Look at your calendar first so you can suggest three specific dates as options.

Chapter 15

How to Approach People

If out of this book you get just one thing—
an increased tendency to think always in terms
of other people's point of view, and see things from their angle—
if you get that one thing out of this book,
it may easily prove to be one of the building blocks of your career.
—Dale Carnegie, *How to Win Friends and Influence People*

He literally spit on my sneaker.

I was visiting New Orleans in my early twenties. Though I grew up in New York City, I wasn't street smart or used to traveling. So when a man approached me and complimented me on my sneakers, I stopped and thanked him. I remember feeling proud that the fine footwear I was sporting attracted the attention of the good people of New Orleans. That moment of hesitation was all it took. Next thing I know, he got down on one knee, spit on my sneaker, and started vigorously buffing it with a rag. I was embarrassed at his generosity until he demanded twenty dollars. Reciprocal altruism, indeed!

I gave him ten bucks and walked away with a valuable lesson: be suspicious of strangers offering too much too soon.

How your contribution will be received depends on how well you know the person and how you present the gift, no matter whether you're presenting it in person, via e-mail, or on Twitter. Even asking for help can be framed as a contribution if you know how. This chapter provides you with guidance for how to approach people, along with three simple exercises to help you practice.

The first step in approaching someone

The reason for the intimacy-level exercise in the last chapter was to help you be mindful of how well you know the individuals in your network. If you offer contributions that feel like too much too soon, you're more likely to evoke suspicion instead of gratitude. *Who is this person? What does he want from me?* We seem wired to quickly calculate whether reciprocal altruism will turn a contribution into a debt we don't want to incur.

For example, if you're an entrepreneur, you would surely benefit from the advice of Fred Wilson, perhaps the most notable venture capitalist in NYC. Now imagine his reaction to your e-mail offering to have coffee or asking him for help. *Who is this person? What does he want from me?* You might as well spit on his sneaker. Instead, you should gradually advance the relationship using the techniques from the previous chapters. You might start, for example, by following him on Twitter and subscribing to his blog. Then you might take it a step further and offer comments. You would be on the lookout for when he posts a question or asks for help.

If you think these small steps won't matter, here are some numbers to show you why they can make a difference. Of the nine million people who have visited Fred Wilson's blog, only ten thousand have commented, and only one thousand have responded to one of Fred's campaigns to raise money for public education via donorschoose.org, where Fred is on the board of directors. An even smaller number of people regularly post comments on Fred's blog. He refers to those people as "the avc.com community." Now imagine Fred's reaction when he gets an e-mail from someone asking for advice. Who would he be more likely to help, someone who hasn't bothered to read what he's already offered or someone who's made the effort to be part of his community?

Exercise: Don't be the sneaker guy (15 minutes)

Go through your relationship list and examine the contributions you've noted for each person. Look for gifts that feel like too much too soon. Then see if you can come up with a simpler contribution. Remember that offering the universal gifts of recognition and appreciation are good ways of developing a relationship without triggering someone's defense mechanisms.

A helpful mindset as you approach people

One of the reasons many of us don't have larger networks is we're uncomfortable approaching people we don't know. Here, for example, is a comment on one of my blog posts about relationships:

> *It may sound stupid, but the biggest impediment to my reaching out to experts I admire comes from a set of tapes in my head that they are too important, busy, and clever to have time for a stranger. I think it's an age and female thing—as my Millennial colleagues have no problem reaching out to anyone.*[1]

Well, I've had that same fear too. *Why would they want to talk with me?* Based on the coaching I do, I find it's a feeling almost all of us share. I also find it's a feeling we can handle more easily with a little practice. Being mindful of the following three questions changes how you feel when you approach someone:

1. What would my reaction be if I were that person?
2. Why should she care?
3. Why am I doing this?

The first question invokes empathy. It makes you more mindful of the actions you take and the words you use. The second question leads to generosity. Framing your approach as a genuine gift is liberating, freeing you from the fear of being pushy or being rejected. The third question leads to confidence. Examining your motives helps you avoid being manipulative, insincere, or otherwise doing something you're uncomfortable with. Seth Godin described it as the "sound of confidence": "Generosity, not arrogance. Problem-solving, not desperation. Helpfulness, not selfishness."[2] If you're generous and helpful as you approach someone, you'll feel much more comfortable than if you're arrogant, desperate, and selfish. That concept might seem obvious to you, but in practice, people routinely come across as arrogant, desperate, and selfish, usually without even knowing it.

In *How to Win Friends and Influence People*, Dale Carnegie analyzed letters he received that showed a distinct lack of empathy or generosity. When I look in my e-mail inbox now, almost eighty years later, I see the same problems. Here are a few actual messages I get from professional salespeople, usually people I don't know who work at companies I've never heard of. For example, they'll routinely frame their requests in terms of what's in it for them instead of what's in it for me. *Do you have time to talk or meet up? I would value the opportunity for a twenty-minute meeting.* They'll inadvertently make me feel as if their time and effort is more important than mine by offering an exchange of coffee for an hour of my day or by fitting me into their schedule. *Let me know, as I have some time over the next few days.* Often they'll simply repeat their self-centered messages thinking that badgering me will change the outcome. *Did you get my last e-mail? I wanted to follow up on a couple of attempts to connect with you.* If those salespeople had asked themselves the three questions before they sent those messages, they would have written them differently and increased their chances of a positive response. As Owen D. Young, an American industrialist in the early twentieth century, said, "People who can put themselves in the place of other people, who can understand the workings of their minds, need never worry about what the future has in store for them."

When Barbara and I were going through her relationship list, there was someone whose work she found interesting but she was reluctant to approach him. The mere idea of contacting a stranger made her anxious. *I would like to know... Do you have time for coffee?* It felt pushy and inauthentic. But with the three questions in mind, she wrote a note based on empathy and generosity instead of self-interest. The e-mail was just a few sentences, beginning with Barbara's appreciation for the person's work and including an offer to help organize an event for his organization if he was interested. She was happy and surprised when she got a response right away. It even included a warm thank-you. "It really works :))" she wrote me, complete with a smiley symbol. "And I was so nervous to just approach him unasked."

When you're approaching someone, no matter how smart, busy, or important he may seem, remember he has needs and wants like everyone else. When you've done your best to put yourself in the other person's position, and you know your gift is genuine, you can be confident instead of afraid.

Q: What if she ignores me? Or rejects me outright?

This is a common concern and has always been a big barrier for me. To help give me perspective, I keep two quotes in mind when I'm about to approach someone. The first is from Seth Godin: "It's arrogant to assume that you've made something so extraordinary that everyone everywhere should embrace it…Finding the humility to happily walk away from those that don't get it unlocks our ability to do great work."[3] When you lead with generosity that's free of attachment, your fear melts away, and you can approach anyone.

The second quote is from Dita Von Teese, the modern burlesque dancer: "You can be a delicious, ripe peach, and there will still be people in the world who hate peaches." Instead of overreacting to one person's response to one of my contributions, I might try again later with a different gift. I may never get a positive response, and that's OK. It's a big world, and some people just don't like peaches.

Exercise: The inbox empathy game (15 minutes)

This exercise is a variation of one from *How to Win Friends and Influence People* in a chapter on empathy:

> *If there is any one secret of success, it lies in the ability to get the other person's point of view and see things from that person's angle as well as from your own. That is so simple, so obvious, that anyone ought to see the truth of it at a glance; yet 90 percent of the people on this earth ignore it 90 percent of the time. An example? Look at the letters that come across your desk tomorrow morning, and you will find that most of them violate this important canon of common sense.*[4]

The modern equivalent of the letters that come across your desk is e-mail. Open up your inbox, and look for e-mails that show a lack of empathy. You may notice you'll see many more examples in work e-mails versus personal e-mails. Write down the phrases that offend or irritate you. The result will be a helpful list of things to avoid when you're writing your own notes.

Q: Why do you keep emphasizing empathy?
At the heart of working out loud are your relationships with individuals in your network. Knowing how to approach people, including practicing empathy, is fundamental to developing those relationships.

How to ask for help

Sometimes you *do* need something: advice, an introduction, a reference. Then what? Even when asking for help, your first thoughts should still be about empathy and generosity. *How will the recipient receive your request and is there any way to frame it as a contribution?* Here's a story from Tim Grahl, who helps authors market their books:

> *Two authors recently e-mailed me for the first time. The subject line of the first read, "Let's meet." The e-mail shared the author's struggle marketing his book and a request for a phone call so he could "pick my brain" about what he was doing wrong and how to fix it.*
>
> *The subject line of the second e-mail read, "Interview." The e-mail was a request to interview me for his podcast*

so that he could share my advice to educate his listeners and promote my business.

Which one do you think got a response from me?[5]

Brain picking isn't an incredibly attractive offer. Before you ask for help, spend time figuring out how the other person can gain something too. It might take some creative thinking on your part, but it will help you stand out and get better results. If you can't come up with a contribution, remember that vulnerability can also be a gift if it's presented in the right way.

Amanda Palmer, a singer and songwriter, spoke about vulnerability as a gift in her TED talk "The Art of Asking" and she later wrote a book with the same title.[6] One of her first jobs was as a living statue. She would stand on a crate dressed as an eight-foot-tall bride and place a hat or can in front of her for donations. Those who gave money were treated with deep eye contact and a flower. Later, as a struggling musician, she often needed places to stay as well as food or equipment. Via Twitter and other channels, she would let fans know where she would be and what she needed. She felt strongly that "you don't make people pay for music. You let them." Why would anyone help her or pay for her music if they didn't have to? Because they got something in return: the chance to connect with her and be part of her journey. Her vulnerability made that possible. Not everyone helped, of course, but when she asked for money on Kickstarter to launch a new album, twenty-five thousand individuals donated a total of more than $1.2 million.

When I needed help with this book—reviewing content, editing, marketing—I thought of the eight-foot bride. I could have pretended to have everything under control, but that would have been inauthentic. Instead I shared early drafts of the book and offered people the chance to help make it better. I sought out people with specific expertise to see if they might be interested in the book's message and helping to spread it. I acknowledged their contributions with personal thank-you notes and thanked them publicly too, the literary equivalents of Amanda's deep eye contact and a flower. Sometimes, when people didn't respond, it stung a bit. I wondered if they truly didn't like me or my work. But I would remember the quotes from Seth Godin and Dita Von Teese, and they gave me perspective. All I could do was ensure my requests felt more like an invitation than an imposition.

Tim Grahl offered some excellent advice for people seeking help from others:

> *When you're in outreach mode, revoke your right to be offended. You're not always going to get the answer you want. People are going to turn you down or just ignore you from time to time. That's a part of the game; that's a part of life. When you don't get a favorable response, take a breath and move forward. Keep looking for ways to help people. Always assume the best of people.*[7]

When the people I'm coaching don't get a response, we practice Tim's advice. We assume the best of people—they're simply busy or have some other legitimate reason—and we focus on what else we can do to be helpful. That mindset ensures your requests don't feel like burdens and makes it much more likely people will respond favorably in the future.

Exercise: The eight-foot bride (15 minutes)

When Amanda Palmer worked as a living statue, she could have simply said, "I would like you to give me a dollar." Instead she found a way to ask for that dollar so that it felt like an invitation and a connection. Barbara could have simply said, "I want to meet you and ask you questions about what you do." Instead she demonstrated her appreciation and offered help.

Look through your relationship list now, and find someone who could help you. Pick someone who's particularly nonthreatening, and practice framing your request as a contribution, avoiding phrases like "I want," "I need," and "I would like to."

Q: This still feels uncomfortable.

The more you focus on empathy and generosity, and the more you do so without expectations imposed on another person, the less discomfort you'll feel. Approaching people can naturally touch on some of our deep-rooted fears and insecurities. But instead of avoiding those feelings, try channeling them into positive emotions that can genuinely lead to contributions to others.

At this point, as you continue practicing to offer contributions and deepen relationships with people, you're ready for more. One way to build on your progress is to consider building an even bigger network and engaging more people.

Key Ideas in this Chapter

- How your contribution will be received depends on how well you know the person and how you present the gift, no matter whether you're presenting it in person, via e-mail, or on Twitter. Even asking for help can be framed as a contribution.

- To avoid triggering a defensive response when you approach someone—*Who is this person? What does he want from me?*—gradually advance the relationship by offering small gifts from the previous chapters: reading what he writes, following him, offering a comment, and looking for small ways to be helpful.

- Practicing empathy and being mindful of your own intentions are the most important things to do when you approach someone. *What would my reaction be if I were her? Why should she care? Why am I doing this?*

- Of course you won't always get a positive response. The quotes from Seth Godin, Dita Von Teese, and Tim Grahl will help you maintain the right perspective:

    - *It's arrogant to assume that you've made something so extraordinary that everyone everywhere should embrace it.*

- *You can be a delicious, ripe peach, and there will still be people in the world who hate peaches.*

- *When you don't get a favorable response, take a breath and move forward. Keep looking for ways to help people. Assume the best of people.*

Exercises

Something you can do in less than a minute
Think of a message you received recently that made you feel more connected to the person who sent it. What was it about the message that made you feel that way? Try to identify how you could use some of those same elements to make others feel more connected to you and make your messages more personal and engaging.

Something you can do in less than 5 minutes
Imagine you receive a LinkedIn connection request from someone, and it's the default, impersonal message provided by LinkedIn:

I'd like to connect with you on LinkedIn.

How would you feel? If you're like me, you might think, "Gee, he couldn't even spend thirty seconds to send a personal message!" Requesting a LinkedIn connection provides an opportunity to practice empathy. You should *always* personalize your request.

Now pick someone in your network that you've interacted with already and send him or her a personal request. If you're still unsure, you can send me a request and put in a personal greeting, mention you're reading the book, or tell me which part you found helpful. I purposefully won't include a sample message since I want you to include your own.

People who reviewed drafts of the book noted that LinkedIn makes it difficult to send a personalized request, particularly from your phone. Great! Your personalized note will stand out even more amid all the generic, computer-generated requests that people receive. It's worth the time to do it well.

Chapter 16

Expanding Your Network

Any one of you could be famous on the Internet by next Saturday.
—Kevin Allocca, "Why Videos Go Viral"

Building your network can take time. Yet some lucky people seem to quickly develop large networks and gain access to incredible opportunities. How? And can you make your own luck?

Consider Paul "Yosemitebear" Vasquez. He's a former wrestler living on the edge of Yosemite whose exuberant reaction to a double rainbow led to forty million views of his homemade video, an appearance on a national talk show hosted by Jimmy Kimmel, and a commercial with actress Jennifer Aniston. There was even a double rainbow song by The Gregory Brothers that got another thirty-five million views. It was so popular it was covered by artists including Jimmy Fallon and, in a sure sign that everything is connected, Amanda Palmer.

There's also Sandi Ball, a.k.a. "cutepolish." She was a student and part-time teacher who liked decorating her nails and, at twenty-one years old, decided to show other people how to do it by making some instructional videos. Four years later, more than two million people subscribe to her videos, which now have over 240 million views. That popularity led to an invitation to speak at VidCon, "the world's premier gathering of people who make online video," where over twelve thousand people attended to meet and learn from successful video makers like Sandi.

Are these just curious flukes of the Internet, or is there something you can learn from how these people built such a large following? It turns out that within their stories are two concepts that are key to helping you find and connect with people relevant to your goal.

Leveraging other networks

One way to accelerate developing your own network is to leverage networks that already exist. For example, Sharon is in my Working Out Loud circle and wants to raise awareness about dangerous substances in the things people use every day. After learning about toxic chemicals in her child's clothes, toys, and furniture, she wanted to learn more and do something to help others. For Sharon, leveraging other networks meant thinking of ways to contribute to the Environmental Workplace Group and to a local support group for two thousand mothers in downtown Manhattan. When Joyce wanted to know more about start-ups, she thought of ways to contribute to the NY Tech Meetup, which has over forty thousand members. Mara, who wanted to relocate to New Zealand, thought of ways she could contribute to the Kiwi Expatriate Association and their two hundred thousand members. When you make a contribution to a large organization, you can become visible to people in that organization, extending your reach.

What could the contribution be? You could start by simply attending their events, publicizing their work, referring new members, and offering help or ideas. Sharon promoted the reports of the Environmental Workplace Group and shared her own research.[1] Joyce started by attending NY Tech Meetup events, meeting with companies who gave demonstrations there, and offering them feedback or publicity. Mara had an idea for improving the Kiwi Association's online community and wound up in an e-mail exchange with the CEO.

You can leverage existing networks when you're just starting out or at any point in pursuit of your goal. In a sense, Sandi Ball's first network was YouTube itself, since there are already millions of women there searching for tips on polishing their nails. Later, when she had an audience, Sandi's videos started including product placements from the cosmetics company Sephora, which then featured her videos on their site. Next, instead of trying to meet producers, marketers, and other experts on her own, she attended VidCon, which had already convened a network of those people. Finally, Sandi's appearance there led to her being included in a story on National Public Radio's "All Things Considered," which has millions of listeners and is how I first heard about her.[2] Each of these other networks allowed Sandi to amplify her work and reach more people than if she only worked one on one.

Exercise: Inter-network (15 minutes)
Play Internet detective and find at least five organizations that are relevant to your purpose.

Q: I couldn't think of any. What am I doing wrong?
It's OK if you didn't come up with any right away. Most of us simply aren't used to thinking in terms of networks. If you're stuck, here's a short list of kinds of networks that might give you some ideas and improve your Internet sleuthing:

- Professional groups like the Kiwi Expat Association
- Conferences and meet-ups like VidCon and the NY Tech Meetup
- Online communities like Jordi's DIY Drones
- Vendors: Many people use a product or service related to their job. The salespeople working at those vendors are eager to introduce customers to other customers or to prospects. In some cases the vendor also hosts an online customer community, making it even easier to contribute.

This isn't a replacement for deepening individual relationships. It's just a way to amplify your contributions so you come into contact with more people and more possibilities. Jordi's online community, for example, brought him into contact with a wide range of people. Over time, he deepened his relationship with Chris Anderson, eventually collaborating with him and ultimately running the robotics company Chris founded.

Usually the network you're looking to leverage is related to an organization. Sometimes, though, it's the network of a single individual.

The law of the few

In *The Tipping Point*, Malcolm Gladwell describes the "law of the few." To make things spread, Gladwell argued that instead of focusing equally on everyone in our networks, we would be better off focusing on connectors, mavens, and salespeople: "people in a community who know large numbers of people," "people we rely upon to connect us with new information," and "persuaders."

Take Paul Vasquez and his double rainbow video as an example. Every minute, another forty-eight hours of video are uploaded to YouTube. So why did a homemade video about a double rainbow go viral? After all, Paul had published videos before on YouTube, and no one paid attention. The double rainbow video was also languishing in obscurity for six months with hardly anyone watching it. But then Jimmy Kimmel, the popular comedian and talk show host, tweeted about it.[3]

Jimmy Kimmel
@jimmykimmel
Follow
my friend Todd has declared this "funniest video in the world" - he might very well be right http://bit.ly/75ieRc
Reply Retweet Favorite More
RETWEETS 467
FAVORITES 147
1:32 PM - 3 Jul 2010

Within a day, views of the video went from practically zero to over 350,000. There were a million views within a week. Jimmy Kimmel's large network amplified the reach of Paul Vasquez to an extent that would be almost impossible for Paul alone. Also, notice how 467 people retweeted Jimmy Kimmel's message and thus passed it along to their own networks, further spreading the video.

You don't necessarily need to chase celebrities and have your work go viral to make a difference. You just need to understand the implications of the law of the few. Putting in extra effort to identify and develop relationships with connectors, mavens, and persuaders relevant to your goal will produce outsized results.

Exercise: Who's your Kimmel? (15 minutes)
Look through your relationship list and identify people in your network who have much more influence than the average person in your list. If you don't find anyone, use the time to play Internet detective again. You might start by looking for people who are already reaching an online audience, paying extra attention to bloggers, authors of books and articles, and other content providers related to your goal.

Q: But I don't want millions of followers.
You don't need such a big following to achieve your goals. I selected the stories of Paul Vasquez and Sandi Ball to demonstrate how even people in relative obscurity can develop

large networks and create opportunities. For most people, the depth of the relationships with people in your network will matter more than the size of the network. Still, leveraging existing networks and influencers relevant to your goal will increase the chances you'll find people who can help you or who will otherwise have access to opportunities that interest you.

Q: Why would people with big networks respond to me?
Because of your contributions over time. Remember the statistics from Fred Wilson's AVC community in the last chapter? While Fred's blog reaches millions, only a thousand or so regularly contribute and are considered part of the community. The contributions over time are what enable you to deepen a relationship with almost anyone. Also, keep in mind that most goals don't require you to connect with celebrities who have millions of followers. Instead, you're just looking for someone who has influence in communities and organizations related to your purpose.

Applying these concepts to *Working Out Loud*

As an example, here's how I'm applying these two concepts to my own work. While I've built a network by blogging, it's small in comparison to other networks that might find my work relevant or useful. To leverage other networks, I'll look for ones related to the topics in the book as well as organizations that might somehow benefit from people working out loud. Here's a partial list:

- Organizations that support human resources, life coaches, and individuals with recruiting, outplacement, and all other aspects of career development
- Groups like leanin.org whose mission is related to topics in the book
- Companies like Jive, Microsoft, and IBM that provide social networking software, since working out loud gives their customers more reasons to use their products
- Conferences that these companies sponsor
- Conferences that are related to topics in the book, such as Enterprise 2.0, which targets corporations, or NMX (New Media Revolution), which targets individuals
- Organizations like donorschoose.org and other education causes that would benefit from me donating book royalties

To take advantage of the law of the few, I'll try to create specific, personalized contributions to influential people mentioned in the book. Some will be the people who work out loud, like Fred Wilson, Brandon Stanton, and Sandi Ball. Some will be people whose own work provided the conceptual underpinnings for working out loud, like Seth Godin and Keith Ferrazzi. If Dale Carnegie were alive, I would send him a copy with a personal note saying how much his work influenced me. Since that's not possible, I'll send a note to the Dale Carnegie Training Company along with a copy of the book and an offer to contribute content for free if they would find that valuable.

When I do this, my mindset needs to be about making a genuine contribution to the network or the individual. If it feels like I'm trying to sell them something or, worse, trying to use them for their influence, then I'll rightly get a negative reaction. My messages need to be personal, authentic, and clear about the value to the recipients. I also need to be free of any expectation that they'll do anything for me or even respond.

Thinking broadly about the networks and influencers relevant to your work and how you might contribute to them will help you greatly expand your own network and influence.

Key Ideas in this Chapter

- Perhaps the best way to accelerate developing your own network is to leverage networks that already exist. For example, contributing to a large organization helps you become visible to members of that organization.

- By the law of the few, some people in your relationship list have much more influence than others. Putting in extra effort to identify and develop relationships with them will produce outsized results.

Exercises

Something you can do in less than a minute
Search LinkedIn or Facebook for groups relevant to your goal. Join one. Or search for "Working Out Loud" on Facebook and join that group.

Something you can do in less than 5 minutes
Make a contribution to an influencer in your network. For example, after mentioning Amanda Palmer in two different chapters, I tweeted this about a video she made that I discovered while doing some research. I wasn't trying to get her attention, but within a few minutes, Amanda retweeted it to her one million followers. It was a small contribution and a small connection, but it made me smile.

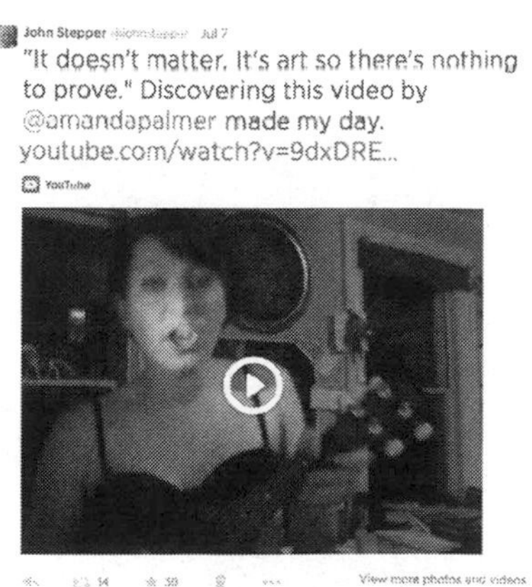

Chapter 17

Your Greater Purpose

The best way to predict your future is to create it.
—Abraham Lincoln

This chapter is a bit different from the others in part III. It's just a few pages long, and there are only two exercises. But for some of you, it might be the most important chapter in the book.

In the Getting Started section, you identified a near-term goal that would help you focus and orient your working out loud activity as you developed new habits. Now, before continuing to work your lists and read about more advanced techniques, I wanted to offer you a chance to take a step back and think about why you're doing all of this anyway. Having a longer-term view will open your mind to some additional possibilities you may not have dared to consider.

A vision of your future

In *Coach Yourself*, Anthony Grant and Jane Greene described a method to help you decide what's important to you and what to focus on: you write yourself a letter from the future. It's a deceptively simple exercise. You choose a date some months or years ahead. Then you imagine what happened during that time if your life had gone well and how you would feel if you were successful and fulfilled. The various examples in *Coach Yourself* showed there's no one right way to write such a letter. The common theme was simply people writing earnestly about what they were doing and feeling at some future point.

> *For it to be real, for it to be useful, you need to engage your emotions. It seems that there is something quite special about writing it down that allows you to reach into your deepest self.*[1]

My own letter

For myself and the people I've been coaching, I found this exercise to be the most effective way to make me mindful of why I'm doing what I'm doing. I first did a variation of it five years ago when I took part in the Relationship Masters Academy. In that class, Keith Ferrazzi had us write up our dreams and goals, a short summary of our long-term vision, and three specific results that would tell us if we had accomplished our goal. He also had us describe how we would feel if we didn't pursue our goal as well as if we did.

I remember feeling nervous when I wrote it. I also remember thinking how odd it was to feel nervous writing something about myself. Yet once I let go of my anxiety and allowed myself to write, I remember feeling that I could *taste* the future. Here's the letter I wrote to my future self:

My Dreams/Goals

To live in different countries for months at a time—Japan, France, Spain, Italy…(to name the top four)

I would like to write (publicly—beyond my weekly work blog, which was at least a start) and to connect with an audience.

I'd like to create! Books but also software and other projects. Things that people would use and love.

I'd like to do something genuinely helpful, particularly when it comes to education for kids who may not normally have access to it. (I benefitted from going to Regis High School, a free scholarship high school that changed my life.)

Oh, and financial independence…Actually, I don't mind the idea of having to work to earn a living. But the dream is more to be able to research/write/speak/ present about ideas and connect with people. Perhaps ideal "jobs" are those of a Malcolm Gladwell, Clay Shirky, or Seth Godin…or Keith Ferrazzi.

Articulating my vision

I will become a champion of ideas. Who will write, speak, and connect. Within ten years. (But taking steps NOW!)

How will I know?

I will have authored a book or other notable content that more than twenty thousand people read. I will have been paid to speak. I can earn a living from writing, speaking, and (only some) consulting.

How will it feel if I don't try and if I do?

If I don't pursue my mission now, I will continue to live my status quo and...my sense of being special will fade. My frustration at not doing "more" will increase. My (constant) fear of having to earn enough for the next twenty-plus years will remain. My entire life will be colored by the two statements above.

If I do pursue my vision now, I will be increasingly happy and... my sense of peace and inner calm will be much, much greater. My energy and enthusiasm will be much higher—every day. My family will be happy because I'll be "present" and happy.

It was four years after I wrote this when I came across the exercise in *Coach Yourself* and remembered that I had done something similar. When I reread my old letter, what surprised me was how much of it still felt right or was already coming true. It seemed as though the act of envisioning the future and writing it down shaped my thoughts and my actions.

Exercise: A letter from your future self (30 minutes)
What about you? What would your letter look like? Remember this isn't your bio or about page or whatever else you might write to impress someone else. In this exercise, write to your future self *for* yourself.

Some of you may prefer visualizing your future self instead of writing about it. If so, try a vision board. It's a collection of photos from magazines or other media that capture what your future self, your future life, will be like. Whatever medium you choose, remember the advice from *Coach Yourself*: "For it to be real, for it to be useful, you need to engage your emotions."

Key Ideas in this Chapter

- Destiny isn't something that awaits you. It's something you create.
- When you visualize your future self and a possible path you took to get there, you increase the chances of realizing that future, particularly when you create an emotional connection to that vision.

Exercises

Something you can do in less than a minute

Go to your LinkedIn profile and add a short sentence about your goal. For example, I added "Author of *Working Out Loud*" after one of the early drafts. Mara might add "Kiwi in London, heading back home." Now when people look at your profile, they'll see more of the real you. That one simple step increases your chances of realizing your goal.

Keep it short. Feel free to try different things till you come up with something you're comfortable with. Then do the same for your Twitter profile.

Something you can do in less than 5 minutes

As preparation for drafting your letter, or to reinforce and refine what you've already written, try this five-minute meditation.

Sit in a quiet place with your hands at your sides and your eyes closed. Focus on your breath for a minute, slowly breathing in and out without thinking of anything else. Then try and feel what your future life feels like. Remember you're not just imagining a one-off event like a party or a lottery win. You're imagining a complete life. Where are you? What are you doing? Who's around you?

Level Three:
Creating

Chapter 18

The Start of Something Big and Wonderful

If we wait until we're ready,
we'll be waiting for the rest of our lives.
—Lemony Snicket

The next level of contributions includes things you make yourself. Just like the homemade pie or handmade card, crafting your original work takes more time and effort, but it's also more meaningful for both you and the person you offer it to.

When I talk to people about creating and sharing original work related to their goal, I sometimes see an internal struggle in their eyes and hear it in their voice. For goals they care about, they may want to do more or even feel they *need* to do more, but they can't. Maybe it's uncertainty and fear that holds them back. Maybe it's because they haven't yet developed the habits they need.

My friend David used to be one of those people. While he worked on technology projects for a group of lawyers, he also harbored a dream of someday writing children's stories. He had plenty of ideas, taking inspiration from the times he and his young daughter, Lily, would walk together and make up characters and adventures. David treasured these moments and wanted to capture them in writing.[1]

> *Everyone, it seems, dreams of writing that one classic kids book; the one everybody reads to their children...*
>
> *The first few lines were written on the train (much like I write these now); a world was forming in front of my eyes and soon it would be a best-seller and life would be richer for it. Except, after about half a chapter I stopped...then forgot to get out the laptop one night. The next I had some documents to read for work...enthusiasm was replaced by procrastination.*
>
> *Soon it was pushed to the back; an idea that seemed like a good one at the time, but probably left to somebody else to make good.*

After that, David's book project sat on his laptop, untouched. Five years went by.

Exercise: If you were David (5 minutes)

Having read this far, you would probably advise David to take a small step, offer it as a contribution, and focus on getting better. Now imagine that *you're* David. What would you tell yourself?

The prisons we build ourselves

If you're like me or like most of the people I coach, the advice you would give David is different from what you would tell yourself. With a friend, you're more likely to be encouraging and supportive. For ourselves, though, too many of us wait for something to happen before we decide to shape our future. We wait to be discovered, wait till our work is good enough, or wait for when the time is right. Too often, we resign ourselves to fate, and then when our dreams don't manifest themselves, we think like David did: our dream is "probably left to somebody else to make good."

But now you have the tools to do and be more. To further increase the odds of "making good," you can go beyond liking and commenting on other people's work and start publishing some of your own work instead. It may seem like a big shift, but it needn't be. This chapter will show you how everyday people doing everyday jobs are making their work visible. You'll also learn about a wide range of original contributions that can help you get started.

Embracing your inner amateur

For most of my life, I associated the word "publishing" with finished works distributed by official institutions. Simon & Schuster and *The New York Times* were publishers. Now, though, we're in an era of self-publishing, and the result is that Sandi Ball and Paul Vazquez are publishers. My yoga teacher who sends me her newsletter is a publisher. Young children making YouTube videos are publishers. You too could publish. But what?

In chapter 7, I mentioned Jane Bozarth's book, *Show Your Work: The Payoffs and How-To's of Working Out Loud*, and the variety of ways in which ordinary people made their work visible. Some people showed finished products, but many more narrated their work in progress. *This is how I did that. This is what I did and why.* One of my favorite examples was a story about Gloria Mercer, a retired schoolteacher.[2] In October 2011, Gloria had surgery on her hand and needed a way to rebuild her strength and dexterity, so she decided to learn how to decorate cookies with elaborate designs. Her first step was to search for information online, where she found YouTube videos, blogs, and Facebook pages that helped her learn the basic techniques. Then she baked and baked, with her husband the recipient of cookies she didn't deem worthy to give to others. She also started interacting with experts online to exchange information.

After a few months, Gloria decided to share her learning on Facebook, sharing what she was doing and learning by posting photos of her latest creations along with comments about recipes and techniques. That inspired her daughter and a friend to also learn, and soon they were all helping each other to improve. Over time, the cookies starting looking better and better, and Gloria started giving them to family members as gifts. Shortly thereafter, her daughter established Coastline Cookies, turning their learning into a new business.

While cookies might seem like a trivial topic, consider the different ways Gloria benefitted from sharing her original work:

- She learned how to post work online.
- She developed the habit of posting and interacting with people online.
- She received encouragement, which motivated her to do more.
- She discovered other possibilities for applying her craft.
- She enjoyed the process while she kept getting better.

Now consider your goal and ways you could share original work related to it. Here are ten examples of contributions that might provide value for people on your relationship list:

1. Share your research.
2. Share your ideas.
3. Share your projects.
4. Share your process.
5. Share your motivations, why you did what you did.
6. Share your challenges.
7. Share something you've learned.
8. Share the work of others you admire.
9. Share your connections.
10. Share content from your network.

As an example, here's a specific list from Nicola, who's in a Working Out Loud circle and has recently started a men's image and style consulting business.[3] If you don't know what that means, you could probably use her services. She'll help you "redefine your look and develop your personal image, giving you the confidence and expertise you need to live an extraordinarily handsome life." Given that, here's some original content she might create:

1. Research: new trends in men's fashion
2. Ideas: how to dress for certain occasions or wear certain clothes
3. Projects: profiles of men she has styled
4. Process: how she works with a client or how she shops
5. Motivations: why she cares about helping men live handsomely
6. Challenges: her own fashion mistakes or mishaps with clients
7. Learning: new looks she's discovered
8. Work of others she admires: recognizing other stylists
9. Connections: stores, brands, and personal shoppers she relies on
10. From the network: testimonials and other feedback

This is just a partial list. You could come up with more original contributions, just like the other members of Nicola's Working Out Loud circle did each time they met. It's as if the toughest part is that first step, framing your work as a contribution and starting the list of ideas. Once you start, you unlock a stream of other ideas and possibilities.

Also, the more you do it, the easier it gets. So here's another example from Alycia Zimmerman, a third-grade teacher in New York City. This list is different in that these items are based on Alycia's actual work online. Some of it is from a public online space she maintains in her name as a resource for her students and their parents.[4] She also leverages a powerful network by writing for Scholastic, a leading publisher of children's books.[5] There, along with ten other elementary school teachers, she contributes yet more original content. Here's a sample of the kinds of things she writes about:

1. Research: resources for teachers and parents
2. Ideas: suggestions for teaching time, poetry, and other topics
3. Projects: dozens of examples of work she does in the classroom
4. Process: how she helps kids prep for standard tests
5. Motivations: why she became a teacher and her values
6. Challenges: packing up at the end of the year
7. Learning: new books and techniques she discovered
8. Work of others she admires: projects from other teachers
9. Connections: people and resources she relies on
10. From the network: third-graders blogged about their class pet

Alycia has written over ninety posts for Scholastic, each one complete with photos of actual work in the classroom, and the work on her own site goes back five years, evolving as she tries new things. The articles are informal as opposed to professional. They're personal, helpful, and engaging in a way that professional articles rarely are.

Why Nicola and Alycia write

The main benefit to Nicola and Alycia isn't popularity. They aren't putting in this effort simply to chase views. Instead, with each contribution, they're learning. Every time they write about a project or an idea, they think deeply about it and get feedback from others. In addition to that investment in their craft, they're deepening relationships with the people already in their network and, over time, creating a portfolio of contributions they can reuse over and over again, unlocking other possible connections.

Remember the two main questions you have in your head as you work your lists: "What's the contribution?" and "Who's it for?" When Nicola writes a profile of one of her clients, she can send that profile to each new prospect or to magazine editors who care about men's fashion. When Alycia writes up a project for her class, she can send that to other teachers, administrators, parents, and other people she wants in her network. Each time Nicola and Alycia write, they have more to offer while making it more likely that other people will discover their work.

Q: This makes sense, but I'm still afraid of sharing my work.

That's a natural feeling. I remember the anxiety I felt when I wrote my first public blog post, even though I knew almost no one would read it. When it came to speaking in public, merely *applying* to speak—just filling out the forms on a website—made me anxious. The almost universal advice for overcoming that fear is to take small steps, get feedback, and keep practicing.

Q: What should I actually do? Start a blog? A Facebook page?
The answer depends on you, your content, the people you want in your network, and even the tools themselves. All of that keeps changing, so it means the answer to your question may change too. A good way to start is to look at people who are relevant to your goal and see what they're doing. Read blogs, like Facebook pages, and watch videos related to your purpose. That will help you discover what you think is good as well as what you don't like. Then emulate the work of people you admire. Over time, as you get better, you'll gradually develop your own style.

Exercise: What are you afraid of? (5 minutes)
Think about something you'd like to create: a blog, a video, a website. Now list all the fears you have about actually creating it for others to see. Try to list at least ten fears or negative consequences.

Exercise: What's actually going to happen? (5 minutes)
Next to each fear you listed, write down how likely it is that fear will actually be realized. Compare those odds with the benefits you'll receive from investing in yourself and developing useful skills like Gloria, Nicola, and Alycia did.

Q: But I don't like writing.
Writing well, like presenting or making videos or doing pretty much anything, is a learnable skill. It just takes practice and feedback. Writing in particular is still the dominant medium on the Internet. Here's a quote that summarizes how important it is:

> *As soon as you move one step up from the bottom, your effectiveness depends on your ability to reach others through the written or spoken word. And the further away your job is from manual work, the larger the organization of which you are an employee, the more important it will be that you know how to convey your thoughts in writing or speaking. In the very large organization, whether it is the government, the large business corporation, or the army, this ability to express oneself is perhaps the most important of all the skills a man or woman can possess.*[6]

That's a quote from the management expert Peter Drucker, and it's from 1952. More recently, Tom Peters, another management expert, described writing as "a timeless and powerful skill."[7] Even if you don't think you're good at it now, getting better at communicating in any medium is one of the best things you can do for your career. As Fred Wilson, the venture capitalist who developed a habit of blogging every day, noted, "The investment I've made in my communication skills over the past eight years is paying huge dividends for me now."[8]

How to make ten contributions with a single post

If you're still uncertain about what you might publish, here's a technique I recommend to everyone: lists and profiles. Simply create a list of ten people or ten pieces of work you truly admire and that are relevant to your goal, and include a few sentences about why you admire them. That list is a contribution to each person on it as well as a gift to anyone interested in those people or in the topic. Here are a few examples:

- Nicola might write about ten fashionable men pictured in Humans of New York or who play in the NBA or are mayors of towns around New York City.
- Alycia might write about the ten educators she admires most.
- Barbara might write about the ten corporate history projects she thinks are remarkable.
- Sharon might write about ten kinds of products that tend to have toxins and point to specific healthier alternatives.
- David might write about ten children's books that shaped the way he thinks about writing for children.

Then for items on that list, you can follow up with in-depth profiles that go into more detail about what it is you like and why. Remember, you're not writing just to get views. You're doing purposeful research related to your goal, refining your taste, practicing ways to make your work visible, and creating gifts for people on your list.

Mara, who wanted to connect with businesses building communities in New Zealand, used this technique to list the top social business influencers in New Zealand. One of the people on that list was a former prime minister who, much to Mara's pleasant surprise, graciously responded. Then Mara wrote up a profile on one of the organizations on her list, and that led to an exchange with the CEO. It also led to ideas for more contributions and more people to connect with.

Exercise: Your top ten (15 minutes)
Think of people or organizations that do work you admire that is related to your goal. Then make a list of your top ten, including a sentence or two about why you chose them.

The start of something big and wonderful

The start of something big and wonderful is, as it turns out, similar to the start of something small and unremarkable: a simple first effort. As early as 600 BC, Lao Tzu understood that "a journey of a thousand miles begins with a single step." Just contemplating the journey or wishing for it won't get you there. Similarly, all the ideas for making contributions won't mean much if you don't publish that first one.

Five years after shelving his book project, David joined a Working Out Loud circle. Between what they talked about in their meetings and the encouragement of the group, David took a simple step: he published the beginning of his story as a blog post called "Once upon a time...," sharing his work for the first time and seeking to get feedback and build connections.[9]

> *I feel if I chronicle the journey of writing it, share that with you, the audience, then this outlet might inspire me to this time see it through. I hope it's fun getting there, and I hope you can join me along the way.*
>
> *So, as part of this ritual I'll post some words, perhaps from the book, perhaps from my scribblings I did and now still do for Lily. This week will be the latter, that original poem about our friend the Tin Can Man. I hope you enjoy it.*
>
> *Once upon a time in a tin can shed,*
> *Lived a tin can man with a tin can head.*
> *A tin can body wearing tin can clothes,*
> *With his tin can feet and his tin can toes.*

Key Ideas in this Chapter

- To further deepen relationships and increase the odds of "making good," you can go beyond liking and commenting on other people's work to creating your own original contributions.

- One of the best investments you can make in yourself is to improve your communication skills, whether that's writing, presenting, or using some other medium.

- A good place to start is to create lists and profiles. For example, create a list of ten people or ten pieces of work you truly admire that are relevant to your goal. That's a contribution to each person on the list as well as to anyone interested in their work. Creating more in-depth profiles of those items yields yet more valuable contributions.

- It's natural to be fearful of the gap between how good you are now and how good you want to be. Just remember that "a journey of a thousand miles begins with a single step," then touch the treadmill, and take that step.

Exercises

Something you can do in less than a minute

Search the Internet for "Alycia Zimmerman teacher" and look at a few of the different results at the top.

Something you can do in less than 5 minutes

Search the Internet for another teacher you know, and compare the results with those for Alycia. Imagine both teachers were applying for the same job.

Chapter 19

Shipping and Getting Better

We work to become, not to acquire.
—Elbert Hubbard

A member of one of our Working Out Loud circles confided that he started writing but, after his blog posts didn't attract much attention, he grew disheartened and stopped. Since only a few people had read what he wrote, and no one commented, he felt like he was wasting his time. "What am I doing wrong?" he asked.

The problem wasn't with his initial contributions but with his reasons for writing and his expectations for a response. The worst thing he did was to stop writing, robbing himself of the benefits of sharing original work and the only way he could get better. It turns out my friend is like the vast majority of bloggers, as highlighted in an article from *The New York Times* titled "Blogs Falling in an Empty Forest":

> *According to a 2008 survey by Technorati, which runs a search engine for blogs, only 7.4 million out of the 133*

> *million blogs the company tracks had been updated in the past 120 days. That translates to 95 percent of blogs being essentially abandoned, left to lie fallow on the web, where they become public remnants of a dream—or at least an ambition—unfulfilled.*[1]

Since that survey, blogging has become easier and significantly more popular. Yet the rate of abandonment is still high. Whether you blog or choose some other medium to make your work visible, this chapter will help you avoid the pitfalls of the 95 percent who don't develop the habit of shipping and getting better.

Thinking of yourself as a risk-free start-up

In chapter 4 on purposeful discovery, I mentioned the lean start-up method that entrepreneurs use and that the same method can be applied to your career. As a lean start-up, when you have a product or service in mind, your aim is to get feedback on it as quickly and cheaply as you can. Then you use the feedback to adapt, ship a new version, and get more feedback. The mindset of the modern entrepreneur is to try many experiments, knowing that most will fail, and use the learning from those experiments to build something people will value.

This is the mindset my friend should have had when he was creating original contributions, particularly in the beginning. Starting with an audience of zero isn't concerning, it's *liberating*. You're free to explore, experiment, make mistakes, and have fun. You have nothing to lose.

Better still, with each contribution—each iteration of the start-up of you—you're learning how to make your work visible and taking another step toward developing the habit of doing so. If you have a mindset that the point of your initial contributions is to get better and get feedback, and you're framing your work as contributions, then you'll be more likely to avoid the fate of most people who start contributing and give up. If, however, your work is simply a means to popularity and money, you're likely to be disappointed.

> *Judging from conversations with retired bloggers, many of the orphans were cast aside by people who had assumed that once they started blogging, the world would beat a path to their digital door.*
>
> *"I was always hoping more people would read it, and it would get a lot of comments," Mrs. Nichols said recently by telephone, sounding a little betrayed. "Every once in a while I would see this thing on TV about some mommy blogger making $4,000 a month, and thought, 'I would like that.'"*[2]

Exercise: What's in it for you? (5 minutes)
Take a sheet of paper, and think again about the lists and profiles exercise from the last chapter. Imagine actually writing up a list of ten people whose work you admire. Think of how you would feel as you draft it and as you actually post it. Write that down on the left-hand side of the paper.

On the other side, write down the benefits you'll get from researching that list, the practice of framing it as a contribution, the practice of writing and publishing. Finally, think of the individuals on that list, and imagine their reactions when they learn how they were mentioned in such a nice way by someone who wasn't seeking anything in return. Picture them smiling and telling a friend about it. Imagine how you'll feel knowing you've produced that reaction in ten people you admire. Write that down too.

For most people, the positive feelings outweigh any negative ones.

Exercise: Your first topic list (15 minutes)
Something many creative people do is keep a list of ideas handy. This way, whenever inspiration strikes, they can capture the idea and have it available for when they're ready to sit down and create. Now's your chance. Whether it's in a small notebook or on an app on your phone, start a list of topics for things you would like to create. You can use the ideas from the previous chapter as a guide, including the lists and profiles. Just be sure to make them specific to you.

Q: Sorry, it still seems too scary to put myself out there.
A bit of fear or anxiety is natural whenever you're offering something, whether it's roses on a first date or a list of people whose work you admire. Still, if the anxiety is so great it prevents you from shipping anything, examine the contributions suggested in the last chapter, and pick the one that feels

the simplest and most genuine. At this point, the practice of regularly making small original contributions is much more important than any individual offering.

The best way to deliver your initial gifts

The astute reader might have noticed an apparent conundrum: *If you don't have an audience, how do you get feedback?* The answer is that you offer these contributions directly to people in your network who might find them interesting or useful. By handpicking your initial audience, you're choosing people who might appreciate your contribution the most as well as people whose feedback would be most useful and relevant to you.

How you deliver that gift depends on your level of intimacy with the person as well as the relevance of the gift. The more intimate you are, the more directly you can approach the person. When Mara posted her list of ten influencers, for example, she mentioned some of them on Twitter along with a link to the post. For others she had interacted with before, she would send an e-mail. Now comes the art of delivering these messages so they will be read and appreciated. Ramit Sethi, author and entrepreneur, captured it well: "You have to sell free."[3]

> *"Sell" has negative connotations, but what it really means is showing people why they should care.*
>
> *For example, do not just send people a book recommendation or random URL. In a world full of thousands of links a day, you might as well send that e-mail straight to the trash.*

Sending people a random link—even if it would change their lives—isn't a favor. It's a burden.

You have to "sell" free. You have to explain why this link matters and what they'll get out of it.

The key is empathy. *What will the other person be thinking as he reads this?* As you keep that in mind, you'll want your notes to have three elements: appreciation, personalization, and value. Whatever channel you use to reach someone, you must show sincere, thoughtful appreciation for the recipient. As an example, let's examine two possible e-mails I might send to Fred Wilson, the venture capitalist I wrote about in chapter 4 whose work I admire. There's a small chance he might mention the book in one of his posts or that there may be some other opportunity, but I'm not expecting anything. Just thanking him directly would be enough for me.

Here's a version that's reasonably concise but would be unlikely to get read, never mind get a response.

Subject: "Working Out Loud"

Hello, Fred.

My name is John Stepper. I work in a large company trying to change how people work. As you can imagine, it's difficult to drive change in large organizations. For years, I often felt like a doctor at a fast food convention: people understood my advice but didn't follow it. That experience led me to coaching and then to creating peer support groups so people could build better networks, careers, and lives. It works!

I just published a book called Working Out Loud, *and I thought it might be interesting to you. You can read more about me at johnstepper.com and more about the book at workingoutloud.com.*

Thanks and regards,
John

I get letters like this all the time from people selling me things. Note that the subject line has no meaning to Fred, the introduction is too long, and most of the letter is about me and has little to do with Fred at all.

Now here's a better version that shows some empathy and includes appreciation, personalization, and value. I imagine that Fred gets hundreds of e-mails each day, so I'll try to pique his interest by crafting a more engaging subject and mentioning an organization he has written about and that's relevant to the book.

Subject: Raising money for donorschoose.org

Hello, Fred.

I've been reading your posts every day for several years now. You've given me an education about technology and investing while inspiring me to do more about education. Your posts about Brooklyn Castle, the School for Software

Engineering, and donorschoose.org made me want to contribute in some way besides just donating.

Last month, I published a book called Working Out Loud *about an approach to work and life that helps you achieve your goals and feel better about work while you discover more possibilities. Think "Dale Carnegie meets the Internet."*

Inspired by the philanthropic work that you and others do for kids, I'll be donating a portion of the royalties to donorschoose.org and education causes around the world. I've sent a copy of Working Out Loud *to your office, so we've raised a bit of money already. :-)*

Thank you for leading by example.
John

Besides the more compelling subject, this short note shows Fred I've taken the time to read his work and appreciate it. Then I made it explicit why he might care.

Exercise: Your letter to Fred Wilson (10 minutes)

I'll send this note to Fred Wilson after the book is published, but I'm sure it could be better. Maybe I could come up with a better subject or a more memorable sign-off. Maybe the smiley face is ridiculous in a letter to an esteemed venture capitalist. So imagine you're me, delivering a contribution to Fred Wilson, and take a few minutes to write your own letter. Try to "sell free."

Q: Selling free seems fake.

I'll confess that writing an e-mail to Fred Wilson will make me anxious. He might hate the book or have some negative reaction to my note. He might not read the e-mail. But I don't feel fake. The reason is that it's a genuine gift, not a trick or manipulation or a stealthy request for a favor. It's just a personalized note showing appreciation and offering some information I think he'd be happy to know. If you don't like the idea of "selling free," think of it as "earning someone's attention."

Q: But what if my contributions aren't good enough?

Although your early original contributions may not meet your aspirations, whether they are "good enough" depends more on how they're offered and the expectations around them. If I pay two thousand dollars for a vase from a store, I expect a certain level of craftsmanship. If my friend is learning to make pottery and offers me one of his first creations as a gift, I'll cherish it no matter how misshapen it may be.

Ira Glass's secret for getting better

My favorite radio personality is Ira Glass, the host of *This American Life* on National Public Radio. After producing more than five hundred episodes of that show, he's won prestigious industry awards like the Peabody and the Edward R. Murrow award, and his program attracts more than 1.7 million people every week. But what's interesting about Ira Glass isn't the number of accolades, his loyal following, or his show's longevity. It's how long it took him to get good at what he does. In describing the process for getting better at telling stories on radio, he said, "I took longer to figure out how to do this thing than anyone I've ever met."[4]

> *There's a gap...what you're making isn't that good...But your taste is still good enough that you can tell that what you're making is a disappointment to you. A lot of people never get past that phase. A lot of people at that point they quit.*
>
> *The most important possible thing you could do is to do a lot of work. Do a huge volume of work...Only by going through a volume of work that you're actually going to catch up and close that gap. And the work you're making will be as good as your ambitions.*
>
> *Nobody tells people who are beginners. And I really wish somebody told this to me.*

Though Ira Glass's work is different from that of Brandon Stanton, Sandi Ball, Salman Khan, and the other people described in this book, they all shared a common path to becoming good at what they did:

1. They produced early work that wasn't particularly good.
2. They produced a lot of work over a period of years.
3. They gradually learned to get better.

I wrote hundreds of blog posts before I was able to start writing this book. Salman Khan created hundreds of videos before he had the idea for Khan Academy. Sandi Ball created over two hundred videos before she would even put her name to her work. Brandon Stanton, the photographer who created Humans of New York, describes his beginning:

> *I was photographing all day, every day. I photographed on Christmas Eve, Christmas, Thanksgiving, New Year's Eve...The first year was really hard.*[5]

Almost universally, our early attempts at almost anything—writing, taking photos, making nail art videos, telling stories on the radio—aren't as good as we want them to be. The only way we can make it past the gap between our early efforts and what we want our work to be is by doing a lot of work, getting feedback, and focusing on getting better. Seth Godin summarized this in a post titled "Actually, it goes the other way":

> *Wouldn't it be great to be gifted? In fact...*
> *It turns out that choices lead to habits.*
> *Habits become talents.*
> *Talents are labeled gifts.*
> *You're not born this way, you get this way.*[6]

Getting better without the suffering

For many of us, thinking about all of the work that goes into getting good at anything is enough to prevent us from starting in the first place. But your path to something big and wonderful needn't be filled with suffering and anguish. The key is to break down all that effort into small, achievable steps. Focus on one contribution at a time, allowing yourself to feel the joy that comes from doing something for someone else. Share your contribution, seek to actively get better, and know that everyone creating anything goes through a similar process. Then use the "change anything" checklist in chapter 13 to help you develop the habit of making more contributions. The stronger your habit, the less you'll need to think and worry about taking your next step.

I watched the first video that Sandi Ball posted on YouTube more than four years ago. Now the video has more than 3.2 million views and 2,500 comments. Looking at recent comments, it's striking to see so many of her young fans mention how Sandi got better over time.

> *Wow you started off just like this and your nail art designs get better and cooler in every video!!!*

> *Omg!!! It is so funny to see how much you have improved.*

> *Watch this and then watch her newest video!! cute polish you're getting better and better in every single video.*

> *She has come a* LONG LONG LONG LONG LONG *way.*

She certainly has come a long way. You can too, one contribution at a time.

Key Ideas in this Chapter

- The vast majority of people creating their own content give up too soon.
- People who produce good work often follow a common path: they produce early work that wasn't particularly good, work on their craft for years, and gradually learn to get better.
- If you have a mindset that the point of your initial contributions is to get better and get feedback, and you're framing your work as contributions, then your efforts will be more sustainable.

Exercises

Something you can do in less than a minute
Look at your list of topics and pick the one that produces the least anxiety, one that might be enjoyable to think about and bring to life.

Something you can do in less than 5 minutes
Now imagine a specific time and place where you'll work for thirty minutes on that idea. Picture yourself in that place, with your computer or favorite pen or cup of tea. Make an appointment with yourself and put it in your calendar.

Chapter 20

Engaging Your Network

We don't just enjoy now, we participate.
—Kevin Allocca, YouTube trends manager

Chapter 16 described techniques for leveraging existing networks and the law of the few. Those ideas and exercises are useful for increasing your visibility and reaching more people because you're using existing sets of connections to expand your own. There's another way to do that though, and in some ways it's even more powerful: find individuals who are emotionally invested in you or your goal and *include* them. When you allow people to feel like they are a part of something, they'll go far beyond simply observing or even using your work. They'll give you feedback that makes you and your work better, they'll build on what you're doing, and they'll share your work with their own network.

When you find people who care about what you're doing and include them, that turns your work into something bigger and more important than anything you could do by yourself. The best way to describe how this can happen is with a short story Derek Sivers told as part of his TED talk "How to Start a Movement."[1] It's about a remarkable three minutes at the Sasquatch! Music Festival in 2009.

The power of the second dancer

A homemade, jumpy video captured a special moment at the festival.[2] It shows people lying on blankets, listening to music, and there in the middle is one lanky guy, dancing by himself wearing only a pair of shorts. He looks as ridiculous as I would look if I danced by myself in the middle of a park, which is probably why a stranger started recording in the first place.

For a while, the first dancer is alone, oblivious to the crowd. As you watch, you can almost feel the discomfort of people in the park as they keep their distance and occasionally glance over. It's awkward to watch him flail about on his own. After an uncomfortably long time, a second dancer joins him. Now it still feels awkward but a bit less so. When a third person and then a fourth start dancing, it becomes a group, something that's easier to join. All of a sudden more and more people participate, each doing his or her own dance, each attracting yet more people. Now a crowd is beginning to form. By the end of the three-minute video, hundreds of people are screaming and dancing, racing from all directions to become part of it. The awkward solo dance has turned into a movement people want to join.

When you view your work as a strictly solo activity, it can be both uncomfortable and lonely. Looking for and enabling others to join you can fundamentally change your work and how you feel about it.

Exercise: Your second and third dancers (10 minutes)
Go through your relationship list and look for a few people who care about your goal. Those people are your second and third dancers, the ones who can help you transform your solo dance into something bigger. They don't necessarily have to be people already close to you, like your spouse. They could just be a fan of your work, a mentor, or a friend who's genuinely interested in your success.

Now think of how you could make them feel part of accomplishing your goal. Remember that even for two strangers at a music festival, the gift was much more intimate than a like or a comment. It was inclusion, an invitation to be part of something.

Q: I'm not sure I understand. How do I find these people?
Look for people who regularly comment on your work or retweet it. Or, if you don't have an audience yet, look for people who ask you questions about what you're doing or who alert you to related work. Those simple acts help you distinguish people who have a passing interest from people who care enough to engage. It may be only one person out of a hundred.

Q: What do I give them?
For now, the simplest gifts you could offer them are gratitude and vulnerability. Be sure to respond and thank them

for their attention. If you've created something, let them see it before it's ready. If you want something, share your personal reasons for wanting it. Exposing your imperfections and asking for help are some of the quickest routes to a more meaningful connection. You'll learn about other gifts later in this chapter.

How I learned that it's not all about me

Looking back at my own goals, whether they were related to a project at work or something in my personal life, my best results happened when I found people who were emotionally invested in the same goal and invited them to be part of it. In writing this book, for example, I struggled on my own for well over a year with little to show for it. Then I shared a draft with two close friends. Their responses? "Thank you for trusting me with this," and "It means a lot to me that you trust my opinion." I was asking them to spend time reading my unfinished work and *they were thanking me!* Their early feedback and encouragement motivated me to keep writing and to make the book better. Over the next year, I wound up sharing more drafts with well over a hundred people, most of whom I had never met and many of whom were complete strangers. Each time, the book became less about me and more about shared interests with other people.

Some of those people, now more invested in the project, helped spread the word about the book because they rightly felt they were a part of it.

Richard Martin @IndaloGenesis · Jun 12
2nd time I have read a draft of @johnstepper's Working Out Loud. It will be a widely admired, greatly appreciated book. Kudos #wolweek #wol
RETWEETS
3
FAVORITES
5
11:16 AM - 12 Jun 2014 · Details
Collapse
Reply
Retweeted
Favorite
More

Richard, for example, went on to make extraordinary contributions, fundamentally shaping the book with his detailed feedback and suggestions. Others helped with everything from designing the book cover to building the website to testing material for Working Out Loud circles. All those contributions from such a wide range of people inspired me to keep trying to improve my work and help more people.

Nine ways to engage your network

Once I recognized the power of inclusion, I started noticing the range of ways other people I admired interacted with their networks. Here's a list of nine different ways you can engage yours:

1. *Respond.* If someone takes the time to comment on your work or ask a question, respond in a timely, personal way.
2. *Let them comment on your work in progress.* Share your unfinished work so people can shape it and feel they're a part of the process.

3. *Let them build on your work.* Encourage others to extend what you're doing rather than try to control or protect it.
4. *Share their reactions to your work.* Highlight some of the things people said or did in response to your work.
5. *Talk to the audience.* The more naturally and directly you speak to your network, the more they will be able to relate to you and care about what you're doing.
6. *Let the audience talk to each other.* Make a point of connecting people in your network, and encourage them to respond to the comments of others.
7. *Show their work.* Showcasing examples of how others are applying your ideas is a way to recognize people in your network while providing social proof that the ideas are spreading.
8. *Invite them to be part of something.* Letting your network know when you're traveling or attending an event and are open to meeting them in person is a wonderful way to deepen the relationship.
9. *Share their stories.* Profile people who have been particularly affected by your work.

One way to ensure it's not all about you is to make it about them. Enabling and encouraging an audience to be a part of your work helps to amplify it.

Exercise: Engage! (20 minutes)

For each of the nine ways to engage your network, come up with at least one example that applies to your work.

Q: That was hard. I couldn't do it.
In a guided mastery program, when you're faced with something that seems too difficult or threatening, simply start with a smaller, easier step. The list above is ordered by relative difficulty. Start by just doing the exercise for the first two items. If that still feels like too much, simply examine how people you admire engage their own networks, looking for things you would like to emulate.

Q: I do respond to people, but then nothing happens.
There might be nothing wrong with your approach. You might just need more contributions and more time. But reflect for a moment on how you're responding to your network. Are your messages personalized for the particular individual? One of the most common mistakes is to respond to everyone in the same way. "Thanks for the RT!" Over time, that comes to feel mechanical both for you and your network, doing more harm than good. Ensure your responses are personalized, authentic, and intended as genuine contributions. The more you do that, the more likely you will deepen relationships with individuals in your network.

Examples of engaging

There's no one set of instructions or style for engaging your network. It can and should be a personal, authentic way to relate to people.

Fred Wilson, for example, speaks directly to his audience, often asking questions or challenging them to debate a particular topic. Then the comments take on a life of their own, going well beyond Fred's original post, as members of the network keep adding to the discussion. Sandi Ball encourages her network to share their own nail designs and offers them encouragement and feedback when they do. As a result, women post their designs on YouTube, Twitter, Instagram, and Facebook using the hashtag #cutepolish. Each time they do that, they expand Sandi's network for her. Both Fred and Sandi often tell people about events they'll be at ahead of time—a fundraiser, perhaps, or a promotional event—offering to meet members of their network there.

When members of Working Out Loud circles made a breakthrough or shared a success with me, I offered to write up their story and share it with my network. I intended it as a genuine tribute to the person while knowing that sharing success stories would also help me spread the ideas related to working out loud.

As I was researching the different ways people engage their networks, I came across a post by Brandon Stanton on Humans of New York. It showed me just how powerful and emotional the connection could become between all individuals in a network.

A memorable example of engaging a network

I cried three times as this story unfolded. It started with a typical Facebook post by Brandon on January 26, 2014. There was a photo of an older man on a subway platform. He had a big gray beard and red glasses, and he was wearing a heavy black coat and scarf. He was looking away from the camera. Beneath the photo, as always, there was a caption:

> *At first we kept saying: "We're going to beat it. We're going to beat it." Then after a while we began to realize that we might not beat it. Then toward the end, it became clear that we definitely weren't going to beat it. That's when she started telling me that she wanted me to move on and find happiness with somebody else. But I'm not quite there yet. Not long ago a noise woke me up in the middle of the night, and I rolled over to ask if she needed anything.*[3]

Four days later, Brandon posted the same photo with an update. "Wanted to share with you guys a letter I got today, because I think it's a testament to the community of people who follow this blog."

> *Hi Brandon,*
>
> *I'm Ted. We met getting off the Six at Grand Central. When I got home Sunday evening, I had an e-mail from friends in Chicago. One of their daughters reads your blog (is that what it is called?) and recognized me even though she has never seen me with a beard. I am astounded! I've read about 1000 of the comments; words cannot express how touched I am by what I have read. It's actually more than touched; it has been very emotional to read the wonderful things people have said. A couple people appear confused about what happened, for the record she had acute myelogenous leukemia, we were diagnosed July 2008, we*

> *lost our battle February 20, 2013, not quite a year ago. Thanks for doing this; it has really touched my life. The most wonderful people in the world read your material and comment on it.*[4]

Over 120,000 people liked the post on Facebook. Thousands left comments. Here are three of them:

> *What I love about this man is that he always uses "we," never "my wife." They both had cancer; they both lost the battle.*

> *I think the best part of the blog is the comments made by people. Their reaction to the posts is just as important in the experience of this blog as the post itself.*

> *Brandon, do you ever have to pinch yourself to make sure you aren't sleeping? Look at what has become of what you started. An amazing community, brought together by such simple things...pictures and words. Finding a new post by you is like a little present.*

Authentic gifts. Talking to the audience. Sharing their stories. Letting them feel like part of a community. Having an emotional connection to something bigger than any one of them. That's a beautiful example of how you engage your network.

Key Ideas in this Chapter

- A powerful way to build your network is to find individuals who are emotionally invested in you or your goal and *include* them.

- Enabling and encouraging an audience to be a part of your work helps to amplify it.

Exercises

Something you can do in less than a minute

Think of someone who has shown appreciation for your work and thank her for it with a personalized tweet, e-mail, or LinkedIn message. It could be a few short sentences like this:

"Thank you for your comments and for being so supportive. I appreciate it. You're inspiring me to keep improving."

Something you can do in less than 5 minutes

Look at one of the people you admire who blogs, and see how he engages his audience. What do you like and not like about what he does?

If you're having trouble finding someone to learn from, look at the Humans of New York posts on Facebook as an example. If you search the Internet for these words—"Brandon, do you ever have to pinch yourself to make sure you aren't sleeping?"—you'll find the specific Facebook post by Brandon that I quoted.

Level Four:
Becoming a Linchpin

Chapter 21

Creating a Movement

In every case, the linchpins among us are not the ones born with a magical talent. No, they are people who have decided that a new kind of work is important, and trained themselves to do it.

—Seth Godin, *Linchpin*

For most of my life, I thought of a movement as something you join, like the civil rights movement, the women's movement, or even the slow food movement. Movements were organized and important. Larger-than-life people started them, not people like me. Then I listened to Seth Godin's "Tribes" talk, and I started to think differently. Tribes are movements, and I mentioned Seth's talk in chapter 5 to point out how it's easier than ever to find or form movements you care about, whether it's ten people or ten million. After all, a movement is simply the process of moving people from one position to another. At the core of any movement is an idea, a quest for change that draws people to it and makes them want to contribute and become part of something. A linchpin is the person who brings it all together through her contributions and connections.

At this advanced level of working out loud—becoming a linchpin—the question for you is "What movement will you create?"

Exercise: What do you care about? (10 minutes)

Take a few minutes to think of issues you care about, perhaps changes you want to see in the world. Better food or education for kids? Restoring a local park? Getting more people to know the joys of knitting? Don't worry about whether it's a grand ambition affecting the planet or a small positive change that just a few people care about. Movements come in all shapes and sizes, and they all need linchpins. Make the list as long as you can.

Exercise: The many faces of change (15 minutes)

Now pick two issues from the list you just created, and play Internet detective. Try to find existing movements related to your issues. Look at sites like change.org for inspiration. The petitions there are typically started by everyday people trying to make a difference. As you find people and movements, start noting what you like and don't like about them. Start imagining how your own movement might be similar or different.

Q: If a related movement exists, why create another one?
You might not. You might just create a local chapter of an existing movement or perhaps a variation of a movement that turns out to be more interesting and effective. Think of a major issue like breast cancer, for example, and how many different movements exist, each connecting people in different ways. For now, focus on what you can learn from movements that are already under way.

Q: All the good movements are already taken.
If it feels like you can't possibly come up with anything new, watch the "Tribes" video again, and take note of the examples. Your movement doesn't necessarily have to raise money for a good cause or fight for social justice, though those are good things to do. You can start with something much humbler as long as it's still meaningful to you. It could be related to your hobby, your personal history, your ambitions, your concerns. The important thing is you're connecting people to each other and to an idea—and that you take a first step.

How the best and biggest movements often start

You can learn important lessons about creating a movement from the story of a brave little girl, Alex Scott. Before Alex's first birthday, she was diagnosed with neuroblastoma, a rare form of childhood cancer. At four years old, she wanted to raise money for her doctors so they "could help other kids, like they helped me." Alex decided to open up a lemonade stand.

Together with her older brother, she raised two thousand dollars with her first stand. So she decided to do it again. Then friends and family opened up lemonade stands, and the word spread. By the time Alex was eight years old and terminally ill, they were starting to count stands in the hundreds. That led to news coverage and yet more people participating and contributing. Now, fourteen years after Alex had the idea to open a lemonade stand, her foundation has raised over eighty million dollars for cancer research, education, and family support.

> *Alex Scott took the "simple" idea of holding a lemonade stand and combined it with the cause of childhood cancer, unknowingly becoming the catalyst for something much larger than she had imagined.*[1]

Alex was a linchpin. She didn't plan on creating such an organization and raising so much money. Her story shows how even the most noble, most successful movements don't always start with the end in mind. They just start.

A simple first step for you

For many people, an easy way to find others who share the same concerns as you is to look inside the organization where you're already working.

Meritxell (pronounced meh-ree-tsell) worked in Barcelona, one of the smaller offices in her global firm, and she cared about empowering women in the workplace. But did the world need yet another women's group? Did her firm need one? Meritxell decided to contribute to a newly created group called enRed—"network" in Spanish. She started organizing events and discovered the women there were interested. The audiences kept growing, enRed became the firm's most popular group in the Spanish office, and Meritxell became a linchpin there. That experience encouraged her to reach out to women's groups in other locations so she could connect them too. Her small first step helped her build a global network inside her firm and gave her new ideas for other kinds of movements she might want to create.

After Mara decided she wanted to move back to New Zealand, she started to meet more people in her company who were also from New Zealand. So she started the Kiwis group at work, an online community where expatriates and current residents could connect to the idea of being from New Zealand. She wasn't sure if the idea would attract enough of the right people, but it only took a few minutes to create the online site. She enjoyed contributing there, meeting new people, and learning what made each of them care about New Zealand. If the idea attracted enough people, Mara could wind up being the linchpin Kiwi at her firm, opening up new job possibilities. Or she might go even further and help other companies create their own version of Kiwis, perhaps even connecting all of them to the Kiwi Expatriate Association.

Barbara, who cared about genealogy and corporate history, took a similar approach. She started by creating an online community to connect all the people who cared about her firm's history. She didn't know how many people would be interested, so she started off small. She might just connect a few other history buffs. Or she could discover that many people cared and were waiting for someone to lead them.

This pattern can apply to almost any idea. Start small with a simple, cheap experiment in your own organization. Learn from that first attempt. Then keep trying new things, refining your ideas until you find other people who are members of the same tribe. As more people join your movement, they help shape the idea, spread it, and connect more people while you keep learning.

I followed this same approach with working out loud. In the beginning, I tried different ways to connect people: one-off presentations, webinars, and lunchtime sessions in the cafeteria. Some attracted hundreds of people, and some I cancelled due to lack of interest. Each small success and failure taught me something new. Then I began coaching people and, once the book was well under way, began forming Working Out Loud circles with people in my firm. That led to events sponsored by employee resource groups where ten circles might form after a single event. Then circles began forming without me at other firms, something I hadn't anticipated when I first started. Other companies started to make videos and organize events about working out loud, referencing my work. A small movement had started.

Q: What if I don't work in a large organization?
If you don't work in a big company, look for other kinds of organizations for people like you and leverage those. Go to where people like you are already congregating, either in person or online, and think of that as your organization.

Then try to create a small, simple experiment to connect people there around an idea.

Exercise: What's your lemonade stand? (10 minutes)
From your list of things you care about in the first exercise, think of a simple way to start. No big events yet and nothing that costs much money. Just a small, cheap experiment to make your idea visible and connect people to it.

Q: Why would anyone want to be part of my tribe?
It's important not to confuse being a linchpin with being popular. While some people do indeed follow celebrities, you're trying to connect people around an idea for positive change. So instead of focusing on finding followers, focus on the emotional connection. Focus on making your ideas and vision so clear and compelling that people want to join you and contribute in some way.

Q: I tried it, and no one responded. Now what?
Try again. Think of what you could learn from your first attempt, and try to frame your next experiment so you can learn something different. Remember the lean start-up model and how it involves many iterations over time so you learn what works and what doesn't. There is no straight-line path to creating a vital, effective movement. It's a meander, taking steps here and there, stumbling and learning as you head toward a vague notion of a destination, a destination that may only become clearer to you as you travel quite some distance.

The next steps in creating a movement

I first came across Alex Scott's story in *The Dragonfly Effect*, by Jennifer Aaker and Andy Smith. It's an excellent book that contains example after example of people using social media to drive social change. From those examples, the authors distilled the four main elements each movement used to drive change:[2]

> *Focus: Identify a single concrete and measurable goal.*
>
> *Grab attention: Make someone look. Cut through the noise…with something unexpected, visceral, and visual.*
>
> *Engage: Create a personal connection, accessing higher emotions through deep empathy, authenticity, and telling a story. Engaging is about empowering an audience enough to want to do something themselves.*
>
> *Take action: Enable and empower others to take action… move audience members from being customers to becoming team members.*

In essence, pick a clear goal; share your stories in a way that helps others form an emotional connection to that goal; and engage and include people, making it easy for them to contribute and make a difference. These are similar to the steps you're taking throughout part III. Whatever your version of a lemonade stand is, your next steps aren't new techniques but instead a shift in your purpose. When you're a linchpin, your purpose is no longer about you and what you alone might accomplish but *what your network will accomplish together*.

As your network grows, so does the set of possibilities
When Alex set up her first lemonade stand in 2000, her network consisted of her family and their friends. As more people offered to set up their own lemonade stands, the network grew, and the family shared stories of stand volunteers and other children like Alex who were dealing with childhood cancer. By 2002 children in other parts of the United States were setting up stands. In the summer of 2004, the entire family appeared on the *Today Show* and other national television programs.[3] At that point, they had raised two hundred thousand dollars, and the goal was to raise one million dollars. That same year, Alex's parents wrote a children's book called *Alex and the Amazing Lemonade Stand.* Two years later, a documentary called *Alex Scott: A Stand for Hope* aired across the United States. Since then, the film alone has raised three million dollars. Now they have important corporate sponsors, while the size of the network, the range of activities, and the impact of the movement all continue to grow.

Ten years after that first stand, Alex's family spoke to the *Today Show* again. To mark the anniversary, they anticipated 2,500 lemonade stands would raise over one million dollars—their original goal for the entire movement—in a single weekend. Alex's mother reflected on how far they had come:

> *I wish Alex was here. She would be graduating from high school next week. But her legacy is something that I think I can't even put my head around. The fact that she has inspired so many people to raise money for pediatric cancer research, but also to do something positive in their life, is really something that's to be celebrated.*

Exercise: Letter from your tribe member (15 minutes)
To help you make the mental shift from what you might accomplish to what your network could accomplish together, imagine one of your tribe members writing to you about something he had done for the movement. What might he say?

There's no pressure to create a movement in your first guided mastery program—or ever for that matter. But all of the ideas and exercises up to this point, practicing the five elements of working out loud, have prepared you for creating one if you wanted to. As Seth Godin says, it's a new kind of work, and you've been training yourself to do it. You've practiced empathy and ways to deepen relationships with people. You've practiced making your work visible—your ideas, learning, projects, even your vulnerabilities—and how to frame all of it as a contribution. You've practiced ways to engage and include people. Now you can apply those skills to a different, more ambitious purpose. The next chapter is about a friend of mine who, though she's only half my age, has shown me firsthand what linchpins can do.

Key Ideas in this Chapter

- Many movements start with small first steps—as simple as setting up a lemonade stand—and iterating, gradually attracting and engaging a network of people who care about the movement's core idea.

- Building a movement is still rare, but developing the skills and habits of working out loud have prepared you for creating one if you wanted to.

- When you're a linchpin, your purpose is no longer about what you might accomplish but *what you and your network could accomplish together.*

Exercises

Something you can do in less than a minute
Go to alexslemonade.org, and browse the site. See how far a movement can go from such humble beginnings.

Something you can do in less than 5 minutes
Now read a bit more at alexslemonade.org/about/meet-alex on how Alex's movement started, including what Alex had to say about herself in 2004. Notice how everything is focused on the purpose, the idea, the people in the movement, and the ways for new people to join and contribute.

Chapter 22

A 25-Year-Old Linchpin

Thank you, your majesty.
—Anne-Marie Imafidon

The story of my friend Anne-Marie shows how working in an open, generous, connected way can lead to opportunities for accomplishment as well as fulfillment. We've worked on the same team at the same company for three years. During that time, in addition to her day job, she created an organization for an important cause, lined up institutional support for that cause from a wide range of companies, and unlocked possibilities most of us wouldn't imagine possible at any age. By the time I saw the picture of her shaking hands with the queen of England, I was no longer surprised at the things she could achieve.

Anne-Marie's smart, but she's not privileged in terms of wealth or family connections. From a distance, she's a lot like other people her age. She has a job in a big corporation. She lives in London with her four siblings and her parents, who emigrated from Nigeria. She hopes to earn enough to buy a small place of her own soon.

Those who don't know her well might say she was lucky to accomplish what she has. Working with her, though, I got to see how she made her own luck. Whatever the task at hand, she would approach it with a growth mindset, experimenting with new things and learning from her successes as well as her mistakes. I saw how she would openly share her work and thinking. I also saw how, when she combined that approach with a sense of personal mission, she managed to create something truly special. She went beyond building her own social network and her own content to building something that was bigger than her, something that had a purpose all its own.

"I want to help girls realize their destiny..."

Anne-Marie's job involves helping people in our large, global firm collaborate using an enterprise social network. In 2012 she thought others might be interested in this work, so she applied to speak at a conference and was invited to be on a panel. A problem, though, was that she lives in London, the conference was in Baltimore, and the firm wasn't going to pay for the trip.

"When opportunities turn up, I like to take them," Anne-Marie said. So she scraped up enough money for a cheap ticket and went. She was heading to the Grace Hopper Celebration of Women in Computing. The keynote speaker that year was Nora Denzel from Intuit who, in a speech entitled "Are We There Yet?," asserted that the number of women in technology had been in free fall for the last thirty years, and the audience needed to do something about it. Anne-Marie heard other speakers at the conference talk about similar trends. Back home, she did some research and found the situation was just as bad in physics and other engineering subjects. She felt she had to try and change things somehow.

Her first step was to write about what she learned at the conference. She had started a blog about ten months earlier, writing on topics as diverse as the Olympics, advice to incoming university students, and women in computing. In her posts after the conference, she started to focus her writing on a particular theme:

> *Women in technology have a duty to use our technical powers for good. To develop apps, to help deal with major societal problems and issues, and to educate future generations so they're empowered to do so too.*[1]

At this point, if it were me, I might have spent a few years toying with the idea and doing some research. Anne-Marie, however, started immediately using Twitter to find people working to support women in technology. Two months later, she was clear on her purpose:

I want to help girls realize their destiny in Science, Technology, Engineering, and Mathematics (STEM) Careers.[2]

She named her new organization the Stemettes, bought the stemettes.org domain name, and started blogging right away. The purpose of the Stemettes was to create "a series of events to inspire, connect, and motivate the next generation of females into long-lasting, happy STEM careers."[3]

"If you don't tell anyone about your idea, then no one else can tell others about your idea."

Anne-Marie's natural inclination seems to be to work out loud. Although she was just at the earliest stage of planning, she published her thinking in the hopes that others could build on it. "I have three ideas brewing. One of which is slightly more formed than the other two."[4] Those high-level ideas included a panel discussion, a hackathon where girls could build their own applications, and some kind of exhibition or conference. From the very first posts, she asked for help and included others to be part of the mission:

> *...we need a core team of impassioned individuals who can offer guidance, advice, their thoughts, and some time for honing these ideas. People who have run events before are very welcome!*
>
> *The initial scope is the UK, but in "working out loud" I hope that others will be able to participate—and I also hope to leverage formats, resources, and lessons learned from around the world.*[5]

Then she took what she wrote and started using every channel she could to tell people about Stemettes: "Hey, I wrote a blog about this with three things I want to try."

"On Tuesday, February 12, at 7:05 p.m. we began the official launch of the Stemettes."
People responded via the blog, Twitter, and e-mail with encouragement and offers of help. That's how she found speakers for the event. Lopa Patel, who founded several digital media and marketing companies and is "an evangelist for STEM," volunteered. So did Rob Johnson, cofounder of a web development training company called Makers Academy that teaches people to code in twelve weeks.

To host the first event, Anne-Marie also needed money. First, she located free space at Google Campus in London. Then, after searching and asking her network, she found her first few hundred dollars of support from companies as diverse as Inspirational You and Impact 10, and also Vodafone, who had heard about the Stemettes event via Twitter and via people in their own networks. She now had a space, some speakers, and enough money to serve pancakes and buy some supplies. But who would show up to this first event of a new group? Anne-Marie had hoped at least a few institutions would appear, and they did. Representatives from Accenture and Bank of America attended after hearing about it via their networks. She didn't expect any girls to turn up, but they wound up comprising more than half of the forty people there. She was happy they had enough pancakes.

In some sense, nothing dramatic happened that evening. No huge crowd; no big news. But it was a step. The positive feedback during and after the event gave Anne-Marie confidence that there was a need for what she was doing, and she channeled that confidence into a second step.

"I would never have thought all of this could be possible before I came here today."

Anne-Marie was getting better at finding funding sources and discovered the O2 Think Big project, sponsored by the European telecommunications company: "We find young people with great ideas and help them get going by giving them the training and funding to make their ideas work." They had already funded over five thousand ideas, so Anne-Marie applied and received the first level of funding of 300GBP (about $450). That wasn't a lot, but it was enough to sponsor a second event, a panel of eight women talking about their STEM careers. More people heard about the Stemettes via Twitter or word of mouth, including Kings College, who helped promote the event. As a result, the audience was bigger this time—sixty people, almost all girls, some of whom also attended the first event. Anne-Marie wrote about each event at stemettes.org as well as on her company's enterprise social network. After reading about Stemettes there, an executive at her firm approved funding for the third event.

Anne-Marie kept trying new things almost every month. Not everything went well. An event might attract fewer people than she hoped, or there would be some technical glitches, but she learned from each mistake and got better. The feedback from the girls motivated her to keep going, like the girl who said, "There was so much keeping your brain going! I would never have thought all of this could be possible before I came here today."

Based on the initial events, Stemettes was now attracting more partners, more girls interested in technology, and more funding. They applied and got accepted for the next level of funding from the O2 Think Big project, which was 2500GBP. They also received 2000GBP from Starbucks and generous hands-on help from a wide range of experts. With this support, they moved beyond events lasting a few hours and attempted their first hackathon, a weekend event where girls would not just hear about technology but experiment with it themselves. Some of the girls, for example, worked with specialized hardware and software to manipulate audio and video in creative ways. There was even a headset that used brain waves to control a helicopter.

"We saw you in *The Times*."

Just six months after Anne-Marie first resolved to inspire more girls to STEM careers, she had organized three speaking events and two hackathons and had more planned. No single event stood out above the others, but she amplified the effects of each one by writing about them and using different social media channels to spread the word. Importantly, by doing things month after month, potential partners knew she was serious, and that led to more funding and more possibilities.

Although Anne-Marie's original plan was to organize a few events, a hackathon, and some kind of conference, the relationships she was building made it possible for her to leverage corporate platforms in ways she hadn't anticipated. Accenture, for example, wanted to pilot workshops to teach girls to code, so Stemettes collaborated with other groups to create the curriculum and run them. O2, a company with extensive marketing capabilities, offered to help with public relations. Toward the end of the year, Stemettes still had some funding left, and Anne-Marie used that to collaborate on a STEM exhibition with a group called Technopop that included 3-D printing and attracted a hundred girls. Not only was it an interesting event, it brought Anne-Marie and Stemettes into contact with new partners.

At this point, Anne-Marie was doing more than just organizing events; she was creating her own network of partnerships. The support from those partners—financial, logistical, and technical—allowed Stemettes to do bigger, more significant things. They were also attracting more attention. Another hackathon, this time with eighty girls, led to a two-page feature in *The Sunday Observer*. The people at O2 used their connections with *The Evening Standard* to place a story there about Stemettes in which Anne-Marie was featured as one of the "Top 1000 Londoners." That attracted the attention of people at *The Times of London*, who contacted Anne-Marie for a feature story and profile. This story, in turn, attracted the attention of people on ITV, who wanted her to appear that evening. "We saw you in *The Times*," they said. Anne-Marie wasn't even aware she was in the paper and had to rush out to buy a copy so she knew what they expected her to talk about.

Anne-Marie and Stemettes were now caught up in a virtuous cycle. More events led to more connections, which led to more possibilities and to still more connections. For example, BIPB, a business intelligence consulting firm, saw the story in the *Evening Standard*. As a result, they offered to fund a hackathon at Oxford for girls to work on data-analysis projects. They funded laptops, a hotel stay,

T-shirts, and even flew in one of their consultants from New York for the event. Bank of America, who was at the first event and was a keen supporter throughout, asked Stemettes to run an event for 150 girls, the largest event yet. It was important to Anne-Marie that the events were always at universities or technology companies or even technology-dependent companies like big banks. These were "all places where young girls would not ordinarily go," and exposure and access to such places was part of the learning for them.

Just a year after her first post on stemettes.org, the group had a mailing list of over seven hundred girls interested in technology, a wide array of partners, and tremendous press coverage. They had done what they had set out to do and more, and all of this culminated in an invitation to 10 Downing Street to meet the prime minister in December. Yet, in some ways, things were just beginning.

"Making it up as we go along"

That was the theme of one of the early hackathons and was meant to help the girls be unafraid of trying things and making mistakes, to empower them to explore.

> *Hack the Barbican really had one simple guideline: make it up as you go along. Be creative and see what happens. And both the girls and I were excited to discover how technology and art intertwined and how their boundaries could be pushed in ways we hadn't even conceived of before.*[6]

But this theme also applied to Anne-Marie and Stemettes. She applied for yet more funding and received 8000GBP from O2 and UnLtd. But what would she do next? Perhaps more urgently, how would she be able to devote the additional time and energy that Stemettes required while still keeping her full-time job?

Here she made two adjustments. First, she used some of the money to hire someone—Jacquelyn Guderley, a.k.a. "Jacs." Jacs was at the first event and had been helping ever since, including writing for the blog and the newspapers. The girls at the events all loved working with Jacs, so she was the obvious choice. Though it wasn't much money, it was enough so that Jacs could commit to spending even more time handling the growing needs of the organization.

The second adjustment was to leverage the institution where she worked. She couldn't afford to quit and didn't want to. So instead of viewing her firm and Stemettes as competing for her time, she looked for a way to craft her job and combine the two. Since an executive at the bank had already supported an early event, and since more people inside the company were noticing the recognition for Stemettes, more executives started to take notice. Because Anne-Marie's contributions, partnerships, and accolades were all visible, it was easy to see that Stemettes was exactly the kind of work the firm wanted to be a part of. The head of the firm's UK business met with Anne-Marie and offered substantial support.

Anne-Marie continued to make mistakes, but they were new mistakes, a natural part of the learning process, and she never let them stop her from trying new things.

Besides the two adjustments she made, Anne-Marie kept experimenting with different kinds of events, different kinds of funding, and different kinds of partnerships. She also tried different ways to promote Stemettes. One was speaking at a panel event sponsored by the European Union. That led to an invitation to speak in Brussels and an article in *The Guardian*, "How can we have more female entrepreneurs?"

The new possibilities just seemed to keep coming as connections and networks unlocked access to yet more connections and networks. Her growing network led to an invitation from Buckingham Palace, where she was surrounded by 350 of the top people in technology in the UK and got to shake hands with the queen. That event, in turn, led to her firm pledging to sponsor an event at the palace—a tech incubator helping girls create their own companies over an entire summer. Shortly afterward, she got invited to a London Tech Week event where other people at her table included Mike Bloomberg (chairperson of Bloomberg and former mayor of New York), Boris Johnson (current mayor of London), Tim Berners-Lee (inventor of the World Wide Web), and Jimmy Wales (founder of Wikipedia). Anne-Marie called it "a pinch yourself moment."

The sound of confidence

By the time you read this, Anne-Marie could be in parliament. She could have founded a new company or continued to do her same job while starting up Stemettes organizations in cities around the world. She may have even moved out of her parents' house.

Success for Anne-Marie and for Stemettes wasn't a neat line of carefully planned steps along a well-traveled path. It was purposeful discovery, each step producing learning, connections, and increasing the set of possibilities. Her story brings to life all the ideas in this book:

- By making her thinking and work visible, she discovered people and her purpose.
- By framing what she did as a contribution toward that higher purpose, she did work that helped others and was also good for her personally.
- By experimenting and learning from her mistakes, she continued to get better.
- By shipping regularly, she created a body of work that was evidence of her commitment and inspired others to join her growing network.
- By leveraging and linking other networks, she was able to scale her contributions and make an even more positive impact that continues to lead to new possibilities.

I'm learning a lot from Anne-Marie. She doesn't seem to have the same fears that I have, that most of the people I know have: fear of failure, of losing a job, of others rejecting her. Her contributions and her network give her a perspective on work that I'm only gradually developing now at age fifty.

I dedicated this chapter to Anne-Marie's story because it could be your story. You don't *need* to discover a personal mission and build a network that transcends your individual concerns. You don't need to make a positive impact beyond what most people would imagine is possible. But you could if you wanted to. You have a choice, and whether the goals you have are more modest or more ambitious than Anne-Marie's, you can learn how to create connections and possibilities like she did.

Key Ideas in this Chapter

- The story of my friend Anne-Marie shows how working in an open, generous, connected way can lead to opportunities for accomplishment as well as fulfillment.
- You don't have to be a linchpin like Anne-Marie, but you could be if you wanted to.

Exercises

Something you can do in less than a minute

Think of someone you consider a linchpin, and do a quick search on the Internet for her work.

Something you can do in less than 5 minutes

Pick one of the items from the list of things you care about. Now imagine you're the linchpin of a movement related to that item. Try and suspend all fear and doubt. Allow yourself the luxury of imagining yourself connecting people and making a difference. How does it feel? Set a timer, and make sure you use the full five minutes.

Chapter 23

Finding Your *ikigai*

In the culture of Okinawa,
ikigai is thought of as "a reason to get up in the morning."
—Wikipedia

I first heard the word "*ikigai*" in a talk about the secrets of living a longer, healthier life.[1] A team of researchers investigated communities around the world that had high concentrations of people one hundred years old or older. The talk was about nine factors that contributed to such longevity, including what people ate, how they exercised, and how they maintained their social connections. One of the locations was Okinawa, a string of islands at the southern tip of Japan, and one of the factors was a sense of purpose, which the Okinawans called their *ikigai.*

When I visited Okinawa in the summer of 2012, I could tell that life was more in balance than I was used to in New York City or even Tokyo. There was less hurrying. Even though the jobs didn't pay as much as they did in the cities, the people took pride in doing them well. They tended to eat local food that was in season, and families seemed more connected to each other.

When the National Institute of Aging surveyed hundred-year-old Okinawans as part of the research, one of the questions was "What is your *ikigai*?" as if that's a natural question to find on a survey. The longevity research showed that, in one part of the main island, there are five times as many centenarians as in the United States, and people live about seven years longer than the average American. They're healthier too, experiencing only a fifth the rate of colon cancer and breast cancer as Americans and less than a sixth the rate of cardiovascular disease.

Listening to the talk made me wonder, "What's my *ikigai*?"

Simple switches in your head make all the difference

As I entered my forties, I had no answer to that question. I just had a nagging sense that there should be more to life. But more what? Money? Achievement? The more I researched my own personal development, the more I gradually understood that what needed to change wasn't my life but *my approach* to life.

Two of the books that helped me included *The Art of Possibility* and *Are You Ready to Succeed?* The first was written by Rosamund Zander and her husband, Ben, a well-known conductor of the Boston Symphony Orchestra. It made me understand that many of my frustrations were in my head, in the stories I told myself. Changing the way I approached the world could fundamentally alter my experience.

> *Many of the circumstances that seem to block us in our daily lives may only appear to do so based on a framework*

> *of assumptions we carry with us. Draw a different frame around the same set of circumstances and new pathways come into view. Find the right framework and extraordinary accomplishment becomes an everyday experience.*[2]

Are You Ready to Succeed? was written by a business school professor, Srikumar Rao. In the introduction, he describes how his early career and life was unfulfilling: "The notion that one could find deep meaning and sustenance from life and from what one did for a living was an alien one."[3] He changed to teaching and began searching through a wide range of texts and traditions, looking for a better way. Then he packaged what he learned into a course that he ultimately taught at Columbia Business School. The ideas in the course are about an approach to life and the way we view it, but he felt those ideas would shape his students' careers as well.

> *I knew I could help them achieve even better results with far less anguish by teaching them a series of simple switches in the way they approached life, such as by focusing on what they could contribute rather than what they could get.*[4]

The books are different in many ways, but they both showed me how changing my mindset—flipping the "simple switches"—could fundamentally alter my experience.

Finding your *ikigai*

Working out loud is also a mindset, and it helped me answer the question "What's my *ikigai*?" My reason for getting up in the morning is simply learning to approach work and life in a more open, generous, connected way. That approach makes me feel better about every day and creates possibilities along the way. It allows me to have bigger ambitions while feeling more peaceful about trying to fulfill them. It makes for a more interesting life.

No matter how old you are, the best years of your life and possibilities you've never imagined may well be in front of you. Not just when you achieve some goal you've been moving toward, but from the practice of working out loud itself. My favorite yoga teacher tried to instill this idea in us as she saw us striving and struggling to achieve a particular pose. She encouraged us to focus on the *practice*, the doing, and pay attention to that without worrying about the outcome.

> *The practice is making the connections. That's it. Making connections that are meaningful and appropriate for you. When you do that, that's when you grow, when you reach places that are more significant for you.*[5]

My sincere hope is that the end of this book is a kind of beginning for you, that as you practice working out loud you'll find your own *ikigai*. Perhaps you'll take a step closer to fulfillment or start a new chapter in your life. Perhaps you'll create a movement or build your own sense of communion with others toward some purpose you care about. Perhaps you'll simply enjoy every day a bit more.

I wish you well.

Appendix

Working Out Loud Circles

Working Out Loud circles are small groups of people who help each other develop the habit of working out loud. Over twelve weeks, through actual practice, you build a network of relationships that can help you with a personal goal. The twelve weeks follow the guided mastery program in part III. By the end of your time together, you'll have developed new habits so you can work out loud toward any goal.

How circles work

There are five important things to know about circles:

1. *Circles are confidential.* Members of a circle will learn better when they're in a supportive environment and don't need to fear being judged or gossiped about. What happens in the circle stays in the circle unless members explicitly agree otherwise.
2. *Circles include two to five people.* More than five people means there's too much free-form discussion and not enough time to provide detailed feedback on each individual's goal and progress.
3. *Circles meet for one hour a week for twelve weeks.* After an initial meeting to get to know the other people and their goals, group members are asked to commit to eleven

additional meetings. Twelve weeks is long enough for people to develop new habits and short enough so the effort is focused and sustainable.

4. *There's a simple, structured curriculum.* The circles use exercises in part III and on workingoutloud.com.
5. *One member is the facilitator.* Groups work best when one individual takes it upon himself to keep things organized, positive, and productive. Like the producer of a movie, the facilitator makes sure things get done: invites members, organizes meetings, facilitates discussions in the meetings, and nudges people who need to be nudged. Importantly, he also makes sure no one gets left behind.

Resources to help you

You can get a detailed circle guide on workingoutloud.com. The guide provides the instructions and exercises you need for each of your meetings. Also on the website are frequently asked questions, stories of people from other circles, and additional exercises and techniques.

Who's in your circle?

Since circles are peer support groups, it's important that members can be open about their goals, their learning, and their struggles without fear of judgment or rejection. For some, that means close friends are a good choice for their circle. Others might prefer strangers. You might include your partner or your boss, but you need to ensure that, whomever you choose, you'll be comfortable being open and vulnerable in front of them.

Before your circle's first meeting

Once you have selected people you would like to include in your circle, it's time to invite them to the first meeting. Be sure to choose a place that's comfortable and conducive to a small group having a conversation for an hour.

The best preparation for your meeting is to read the book. If you don't have time to finish it, read the beginning of part III "Your Guided Mastery Program," including chapter 10, "A Practical Goal and Your First Relationship List." Everyone in the circle should also read the circle guide and bring it to the first meeting.

Circles inside your company

Forming circles can also be an employee-centered, self-organizing, free way to create a more open, collaborative culture in any organization. Here are the three most important things you would need to know about implementing circles in your organization:

1. *Circles are employee driven.* It's key that employees choose to participate, work on a goal that's important to them, and trust that what happens inside the circle is confidential. If you impose manager approval or reporting requirements, you won't realize the benefits.

2. *Circles are open to anyone.* Since circle members will be practicing basic twenty-first-century skills, access should not be restricted to only those with a certain title or those deemed to have potential. The most important criterion is the willingness to make an effort to learn.
3. *Circles meet twelve times for one hour.* These meetings could be outside normal business hours if necessary, depending on the organization. Individuals will also need to do work related to their goal in between meetings.

People could form circles outside of their company, of course. But forming circles inside a company has a number of advantages. The people there already have much in common, making it easier to form connections and even exchange their circle experiences. Also, if the organization uses an enterprise social network like Jive, Yammer, IBM Connections, Socialcast, Podio, or similar offering, people will have a convenient platform to work out loud. Employees who work out loud at work are personally more effective, help the firm capture knowledge, and make it easier for others to access that knowledge.

The role of management

While the circles are employee centered and the resources I mentioned are free, there are things that management could do to help. For example, by endorsing circles as an employee development offering or promoting them at employee networking events, they would remove any doubts about whether employees are allowed to form them. Executives could also ensure there is time to participate in them, reducing possible interference from middle managers. Managers at all levels could motivate more people to participate by sharing stories of individuals and teams that are working out loud for their own benefit and that of the company.

If you were to describe someone who worked out loud, you might say she's visible, connected, generous, curious, and purposeful. The circles would help your employees to feel like that, to *be* like that. The practice over time and the peer support would enable people to finally break free of old ways of working and of thinking about work. They could finally develop new habits at work that tap into the intrinsic motivators of autonomy, purpose, mastery, and relatedness. Doing so in a visible way, together with the support of the firm, would accelerate the spread of these positive behaviors across the organization, changing the culture.

At a minimum, some circle members might learn to more readily search for people and content related to their work. Many will build a larger set of more meaningful relationships at work, enabling them to collaborate more effectively. Still others will feel like Barbara when she wrote that "working out loud changed my life." Combined, all that learning would fundamentally change how people relate to each other and to the organization.

Additional Reading

I love books. One of my great joys is opening up a book for the first time and immersing myself in it. Here's a short list of books I recommend that are related in some way to working out loud. You can find other books I recommend on goodreads.com.

A world view

If you only pick two books from this list, pick these two. They are a joy to read, and they are the most broadly applicable. While I had always thought of myself as a positive person, these books freed me to be more joyful and more open to the wonders in other people:

> *Are You Ready to Succeed? Unconventional Strategies to Achieving Personal Mastery in Business and Life*, by Srikumar Rao
>
> *The Art of Possibility: Transforming Professional and Personal Life*, by Rosamund Stone Zander and Ben Zander

New approaches to basic skills

These four books helped me rethink how I make my work visible. With their help and a lot of practice, I've become better at these fundamental skills, and I'm convinced anyone can do the same:

On Writing Well: The Classic Guide to Writing Nonfiction, by William Zinsser

Reading Like a Writer: A Guide for People Who Love Books and for Those Who Want to Write Them, by Francine Prose

Presentation Zen: Simple Ideas on Presentation Design and Delivery, by Garr Reynolds

Resonate: Present Visual Stories that Transform Audiences, by Nancy Duarte

Developing relationships

These books made me think more deeply about what people need and want in relationships and how I could apply that in building a network to accomplish something:

How to Win Friends and Influence People: The Only Book You Need to Lead You to Success, by Dale Carnegie

Never Eat Alone: And Other Secrets to Success, One Relationship at a Time, by Keith Ferrazzi with Tahl Raz

Who's Got Your Back: The Breakthrough Program to Build Deep, Trusting Relationships that Create Success—and Won't Let You Fail, by Keith Ferrazzi

Personal productivity and creativity

These books, shorter and easier to read than the others, gave me a new perspective on how people create great work:

Manage Your Day-to-Day: Build Your Routine, Find Your Focus, and Sharpen Your Creative Mind, edited by Jocelyn Glei

Maximize Your Potential: Grow Your Expertise, Take Bold Risks & Build an Incredible Career, edited by Jocelyn Glei

Steal Like an Artist: 10 Things Nobody Told You About Being Creative, by Austin Kleon

Show Your Work!: 10 Ways to Share Your Creativity and Get Discovered, by Austin Kleon

Show Your Work: The Payoffs and How-To's of Working Out Loud, by Jane Bozarth

Thinking about thinking

Having a better understanding of how your mind works is perhaps the most empowering knowledge you can have. These books made it possible for me to control more of my thoughts rather than have them control me:

Thinking, Fast and Slow, by Daniel Kahneman

Your Brain at Work: Strategies for Overcoming Distraction, Regaining Focus, and Working Smarter All Day Long, by David Rock

Self-Esteem: A Proven Program of Cognitive Techniques for Assessing, Improving, and Maintaining Your Self-Esteem, by Matthew McKay and Patrick Fanning

Why we do what we do—and how to change it

These books helped me understand what generally motivates people and how to change my habits. They also empowered me to actively shape my future instead of watching it unfold:

Flow: The Psychology of Optimal Experience, by Mihaly Csikszentmihalyi

Drive: The Surprising Truth About What Motivates Us, by Daniel Pink

The Willpower Instinct: How Self-Control Works, Why It Matters, and What You Can Do to Get More of It, by Kelly McGonigal

Driving larger-scale changes

Whether you're trying to change your firm, change your local community, or change the world, these book offer approaches, frameworks, and heroic examples that will inspire you and make you more effective:

The Lean Startup: How Today's Entrepreneurs Use Continuous Innovation to Create Radically Successful Businesses, by Eric Ries

Influencer: The Power to Change Anything, by Kerry Patterson, Joseph Grenny, David Maxfield, Ron McMillan, and Al Switzler

The Dragonfly Effect: Quick, Effective, and Powerful Ways to Use Social Media to Drive Social Change, by Jennifer Aaker and Andy Smith, with Carlye Adler

Switch: How to Change Things When Change Is Hard, by Chip Heath and Dan Heath

Linchpin: Are You Indispensable?, by Seth Godin

Mountains Beyond Mountains: The Quest of Dr. Paul Farmer, a Man Who Would Cure the World, by Tracy Kidder

The Blue Sweater: Bridging the Gap Between Rich and Poor in an Interconnected World, by Jaqueline Novogratz

Whatever It Takes: Geoffrey Canada's Quest to Change Harlem and America, by Paul Tough

Finding happiness

The insights found in this eclectic mix of books allowed me to see the limitations I had placed on myself. They showed me the different ways I was actively making myself unhappy and how to change that:

Be Free Where You Are, by Thich Nhat Hanh

Peace Is Every Step: The Path of Mindfulness in Everyday Life, by Thich Nhat Hanh

A New Earth: Awakening to Your Life's Purpose, by Eckhart Tolle

Steering by Starlight: The Science and Magic of Finding Your Destiny, by Martha Beck

The Happiness Project: Or, Why I Spent a Year Trying to Sing in the Morning, Clean My Closets, Fight Right, Read Aristotle, and Generally Have More Fun, by Gretchen Rubin

Notes

Chapter 1: Four Stories

1 Albert Sabate, "Jordi Muñoz Wants You to Have a Drone of Your Own," February 1, 2013, http://abcnews.go.com/ABC_Univision/News/jordi-muoz-drone/story?id=18332163.

2 Chris Anderson, *Makers* (New York: Crown Business, 2012): 146.

3 CNBC, Laura Hill and Joyce Sullivan, March 5, 2010, video.cnbc.com/gallery/?video=1432799925.

4 Barbara Schmidt, "A Whole New World," February 8, 2014, http://schmidtbarbara.wordpress.com/2014/02/08/a-whole-new-world/.

5 From personal correspondence that Barbara shared with me.

6 Barbara Schmidt, "My Work Out Loud (WOL) Journey," July 7, 2014, http://schmidtbarbara.wordpress.com/2014/07/07/my-work-out-loud-wol-journey/.

Chapter 2: Improving Your Odds

1 Amy Wrzesniewski, Clark McCauley, Paul Rozin, and Barry Schwartz, "Jobs, Careers, and Callings: People's Relations to Their Work," *Journal of Research in Personality* 31, (1997): 21–33.

2 Ibid.

3 Daniel Pink, *Drive* (New York: Riverhead Books, 2011): 76.

4 Mihaly Czikszentmihalyi, *Flow* (New York: Harper Perennial Modern Classics, 2008), xi.

5 Ibid., 2.

6 Tony Schwartz and Christine Porath, "Why You Hate Work," *New York Times*, May 30, 2014, http://www.nytimes.com/2014/06/01/opinion/sunday/why-you-hate-work.html.

7 Maddie Grant and Jamie Notter, *Humanize* (Indianapolis: Que Publishing, 2011), 58.

8 Susan Sorenson, "How Employee Engagement Drives Growth," *Gallup Business Journal*, June 20, 2013, http://www.gallup.com/businessjournal/163130/employee-engagement-drives-growth.aspx.

9 Amy Wrzesniewski and Jane E. Dutton, "Crafting a Job: Revisioning Employees as Active Crafters of Their Work," *Academy of Management Review* 26, no. 2 (2001): 179–201.

10 Ibid.

11 Ibid.

12 Mark Granovetter, "The Strength of Weak Ties," *American Journal of Sociology* 78, no. 6 (May 1973): 1360–80.

13 Ibid., 1372.

1 Bryce Williams, "When Will We Work Out Loud? Soon!" November 29, 2010, thebryceswrite.com/2010/11/29/when-will-we-work-out-loud-soon/.

Chapter 4: Purposeful Discovery

1 Alain de Botton, *The Pleasures and Sorrows of Work* (New York: Vintage, 2010): 113.

2 Brandon Stanton, "Humans of New York: Behind the Lens," *Huffington Post*, May 3, 2013, huffingtonpost.com/brandon-stanton/humans-of-new-york-behind_b_3210673.html.

3 Sarah Goodyear, "A 'Photographic Census' Captures New York's Characters," *The Atlantic Citylab*, April 20, 2012, http://www.citylab.com/design/2012/04/photographic-census-captures-new-yorks-characters/1816/.

4 Stanton, "Humans of New York: Behind the Lens."

5 Brandon Stanton, "I am Brandon Stanton, creator of the Humans of New York blog. I've stopped, photographed, and interviewed

thousands of strangers on the streets of NYC," http://www.reddit.com/r/IAmA/comments/1eq6cm/i_am_brandon_stanton_creator_of_the_humans_of_new/.

6 Humans of New York, "We told her to sit with us so we could share her sadness," August 8, 2014, https://www.facebook.com/humansofnewyork/photos/a.102107073196735.4429.102099916530784/739242252816544/?type=1&theater.

7 Reid Hoffman and Ben Casnoch, *The Start-up of You* (New York: Crown Business, 2012): jacket, 40.

8 Eric Ries, *Lean Startup* (New York: Crown Business, 2011).

Chapter 5: Building Relationships

1 Ibid., 31.

2 Dale Carnegie, *How to Win Friends and Influence People* (New York: Pocket Books, 2010).

3 Ronald Burt, *Structural Holes: The Social Structure of Competition* (Cambridge, MA: Harvard University Press, 1995).

4 An online version of Keith Ferrazzi's course used to be available at mygreenlight.com but they are no longer accepting enrollments.

5 Keith Ferrazzi, *Who's Got Your Back?* (New York: Crown Business, 2009): 41.

6 Duncan Watts and Steven H. Strogatz, "Collective Dynamics of 'Small-World' Networks," *Nature* 393, no. 4 (June 1998): 440–2.

7 In a group of twenty-five people, for example, the most robust network might be to have everyone know everyone else, but that would require three hundred connections. You could get most of the networking benefits with a fifth of those connections by forming five densely connected groups (ten connections each) and having a few people who are members of multiple groups.

8 Seth Godin, *Tribes* (New York: Portfolio Hardcover, 2008): 1.

9 Seth Godin, "The Tribes We Lead," February 2009, ted.com/talks/seth_godin_on_the_tribes_we_lead.html

10 http://hbr.org/2005/12/how-to-build-your-network/ar/1.

11 Godin, *Tribes*, 4.

14 Here's one of many examples out there: Julie Bort, "17 New Ways to Make Your LinkedIn Profile Irresistible to Employers," October 17, 2013, http://www.businessinsider.com/make-your-linkedin-profile-irresistible-2013-10?op=1.

Chapter 6: Leading with Generosity

1 Meredith P. Crawford, "The Cooperative Solving of Problems by Young Chimpanzees," *Comparative Psychology Monographs* 14 (1937).

2 Robert L. Trivers, "The Evolution of Reciprocal Altruism," *The Quarterly Review of Biology* 46, no. 1 (March 1971): 35–57.

3 Frans B. M. de Waal, Kristin Leimgruber, and Amanda R. Greenberg, "Giving Is Self-Rewarding for Monkeys," *Proceedings of the National Academy of Sciences* 105, no. 36 (July 2008).

4 Adam Grant, *Give and Take* (New York: Penguin Books, 2014): 157.

5 Fred Wilson, "Writing It Down," September 19, 2013, avc.com/a_vc/2013/09/writing-it-down.html.

6 Fred Wilson, "The Academy for Software Engineering," January 13, 2012, http://avc.com/2012/01/the-academy-for-software-engineering/.

7 Reid Hoffman, "Connections with Integrity," *Strategy + business* 67 (May 29, 2012), http://www.strategy-business.com/article/00104?pg=all.

8 Keith Ferrazzi, *Never Eat Alone* (New York: Crown Business, 2005): 21.

Chapter 7: Making You and Your Work Visible

1 Andrew McAfee, "Do's and Don'ts for Your Work's Social Platforms," *Harvard Business Review*, September 28, 2010, https://hbr.org/2010/09/dos-and-donts-for-your-works-s/.

2 Dave Winer, "Narrate Your Work," August 9, 2009, http://scripting.com/stories/2009/08/09/narrateYourWork.html.

3 Brian Tullis, "Observable Flow: The Taming of the Flow," June 25, 2010, http://nextthingsnext.blogspot.com/2010/06/observable-work-taming-of-flow.html.

4 Williams, "When Will We Work Out Loud? Soon!"

5 James Manyika, Michael Chui, and Hugo Sarrazin, "Social Media's Productivity Payoff," *McKinsey Global Institute*, August 21, 2012, mckinsey.com/insights/mgi/in_the_news/social_media_productivity_payoff.

6 Ibid.

7 Karen Renaud, Judith Ramsay, and Mario Hair, "'You've Got E-Mail!'...Shall I Deal with It Now? Electronic Mail from the Recipient's Perspective," *International Journal of Human-Computer Interaction* 21, no. 3 (2006): 313–32.

8 Bill French, "Email Is Where Knowledge Goes to Die," February 28, 2011, http://ipadcto.com/2011/02/28/email-is-where-knowledge-goes-to-die/.

9 The collaboration platform is based on Jive software. You can learn more about it at https://www.jivesoftware.com.

10 Jane Bozarth, *Show Your Work* (San Francisco: Pfeiffer, 2014).

Chapter 8: A Growth Mindset

1 Claudia M. Mueller and Carol S. Dweck, "Praise for Intelligence Can Undermine Children's Motivation and Performance," *Journal of Personality and Social Psychology* 75, no. 1 (1998): 33–52.

2 Albert Bandura, Edward B. Blanchard, and Brunjilde Ritter, "Relative efficacy of desensitization and modeling approaches for inducing behavioral, affective, and attitudinal changes," *Journal of Personality and Social Psychology*, 13, no. 3 (1969): 173–99.

3 Ibid., 197.

4 Albert Bandura, "Self-efficacy," in *Encyclopedia of Human Behavior 4*, ed. V. S. Ramachaudran (New York: Academic Press, 1994): 71–81.

5 khanacademy.org/about

6 Salman Khan, "Let's Use Video to Reinvent Education," March 2011, http://www.ted.com/talks/salman_khan_let_s_use_video_to_reinvent_education.

7 Jocelyn Glei, ed. *Maximize Your Potential: Grow Your Expertise, Take Bold Risks & Build an Incredible Career* (Las Vegas: Amazon Publishing, 2013): 79.

8 Ibid., 81.

9 Albert Bandura, "Cultivate Self-Efficacy for Personal and Organizational Effectiveness," in *Handbook of principles of organization behavior*, E. A. Locke, ed. (Oxford, UK: Blackwell, 2000): 120–36.

Chapter 11: Your First Contributions

1 Scott Berkun, "#49–How to Make a Difference," October 2008, http://scottberkun.com/essays/ 49-how-to-make-a-difference/.

Chapter 12: Working Your Lists

1 George S. Clason, *The Richest Man in Babylon* (New York: Signet 2002): 3.

2 Ibid., 13.

3 Ibid., 20.

4 TV is just one example of how we spend our leisure time. For more statistics on TV viewing by age group, see this Nielsen report: http://www.nielsen.com/content/dam/corporate/us/en/newswire/uploads/2011/04/State-of-the-Media-2011-TV-Upfronts.pdf.

Chapter 13: Making It a Habit

1 Daniel Kahneman, *Thinking, Fast and Slow* (New York: Farrar, Straus and Giroux, 2013).

2 Tony Grant and Jane Greene, *Coach Yourself* (New York: Basic Books, 2003).

3 Karen Pryor, *Don't Shoot the Dog* (New York: Bantam, 1999).

Chapter 15: How to Approach People

1 Comment on http://johnstepper.com/2014/01/25/approaching-people-who-are-smarter-busier-and-more-important-than-you/.

2 Seth Godin, "The Sound of Confidence," November 23, 2013, http://sethgodin.typepad.com/seths_blog/2013/11/the-sound-of-confidence.html.

3 Seth Godin, "The Humility of the Artist," January 19, 2014, http://sethgodin.typepad.com/seths_blog/2014/01/the-humility-of-the-artist.html.

4 Carnegie, *How to Win Friends and Influence People*, 6.

5 Tim Grahl, *Your First 1000 Copies* (Lynchburg, VA: Out:think, 2013): 84.

6 Amanda Palmer, "The Art of Asking," 2013, http://www.ted.com/talks/amanda_palmer_the_art_of_asking. The book came out in 2014. Amanda Palmer, *The Art of Asking*, (New York: Grand Centeal Publishing, 2014).

7 Grahl, *Your First 1000 Copies*, 87.

Chapter 16: Expanding Your Network

1 Mama Scoop, https://www.facebook.com/groups/146359561721627 4/

2 Corey Takahashi, "At VidCon, a Chance to See YouTube Celebrities off the Screen," June 28, 2014, http://www.npr.org/2014/06/28/326406753/the-underground-rock-stars-of-vidcon.

3 Allocca, "Why Videos Go Viral."

Chapter 17: Your Greater Purpose

1 Grant and Greene, *Coach Yourself*, 17.

Chapter 18: The Start of Something Big and Wonderful

1 David Griffin, "Once Upon a Time," January 30, 2013, http://tellinstoriesblog.wordpress.com/2013/01/30/once-upon-a-time/.

2 Bozarth, *Show Your Work*, 62. Note that it was adapted from an article that first appeared in *Learning Solutions* magazine.

3 89http://www.harrison-style.com/

4 90 http://www.alyciazimmerman.com

5 http://www.scholastic.com/teachers/teaching-ideas/alycia-zimmerman

6 Peter Drucker, "How to Be an Employee," May 1952, *Fortune*.

7 Tom Peters, "Brand You Thoughts from Tom Peters: Work on Your Writing," January 21, 2010, https://www.youtube.com/watch?v=EEHLHdoPfWA.

8 Fred Wilson, "Writing," November 22, 2011, http://www.avc.com/a_vc/2011/11/writing.html.

9 Griffin, "Once Upon a Time," https://tellinstoriesblog.wordpress.com/2013/01/30/once-upon-a-time/.

Chapter 19: Shipping and Getting Better

1 Douglas Quenqua, "Blogs Falling in an Empty Forest," *New York Times*, June 5, 2009, http://www.nytimes.com/2009/06/07/fashion/07blogs.html.
2 Ibid.
3 Ramit Sethi, "How This Guy Can Get People to Read His E-mails," July 28, 2014, http://www.iwillteachyoutoberich.com/blog/how-this-guy-can-get-people-to-read-his-e-mails/.
4 PRI Public Radio International, "Ira Glass on Storytelling, part 2 of 4," August 18, 2009, http://www.youtube.com/watch?v=KW6x7lOIsPE#t=22.
5 Chloe Pantazi, "The Power of One Human of New York," October 15, 2013, http://hyperallergic.com/88335/the-power-of-one-human-of-new-york/.
6 Seth Godin, "Actually, It Goes the Other Way," February 22, 2013, http://sethgodin.typepad.com/seths_blog/2013/02/goestheother-way.html.

Chapter 20: Engaging Your Network

1 Derek Sivers, "How to Start a Movement," February 2010, http://www.ted.com/talks/derek_sivers_how_to_start_a_movement.
2 Dkellerm, "Sasquatch Music Festival 2009—Guy Starts Dance Party, May 26, 2009 https://www.youtube.com/watch?v=GA8z7f7a2Pk.
3 Humans of New York, "At first we kept saying, 'We're going to beat it. We're going to beat it,'" January 26, 2014, http://www.humansofnewyork.com/post/74684588041/at-first-we-kept-saying-were-going-to-beat-it.

4 Humans of New York, "I wanted to share with you guys a letter I got today," January 31, 2014, http://www.humansofnewyork.com/post/75156150700/wanted-to-share-with-you-guys-a-letter-i-got.

Chapter 21: Creating a Movement

1 http://www.alexslemonade.org

2 Jennifer Aaker and Andy Smith, *The Dragonfly Effect* (San Francisco: Jossey-Bass, 2010): 9.

3. Alex and her family appearing on the *Today Show* with Matt Lauer in June 2004: http://www.today.com/video/today/5136668#5136668.

Chapter 22: A 25-Year-Old Linchpin

1 Anne-Marie Imafidon, "The Case for Women Leadership in Technology and Beyond—My Month on the East Coast," October 31, 2012, http://aimafidon.com/2012/10/31/the-case-for-women-leadership-in-technology-and-beyond-my-month-on-the-east-coast/.

2 Anne-Marie Imafidon, "For 2013: 3 New Years Resolutions I Won't Have and 1 New Years Objective I Do Have," December 31, 2012, http://aimafidon.com/2012/12/31/for-2013-3-new-years-resolutions-i-wont-have-and-1-new-years-objective-i-do-have/.

3 Ibid.

4 Ibid.

5 Ibid.

6 Stemettes, "'Making It Up as We Go Along'—Stemettes Hack the Barbican," May 13, 2013, https://stemettes.wordpress.com/2013/05/13/making-it-up-as-we-go-along-stemettes-hack-the-barbican/.

Chapter 23: Finding Your ikigai

1 Dan Buettner, "How to Live to Be 100+," September 2009, http://www.ted.com/talks/dan_buettner_how_ to_live_to_be_100.

2 Rosamund Stone Zander and Benjamin Zander, *The Art of Possibility* (New York: Penguin Books, 2002): 1.

3 Srikumar S. Rao, *Are Your Ready to Succeed?* (New York: Hyperion, 2006): 3.

4 Ibid., 5.

5 You can find more wisdom from my yoga teacher, Mindy, on her website at http://mindybacharach.com.

Acknowledgments

Hundreds of people shaped this book and provided support and inspiration. The first person to see any part of the book was Moyra Mackie, and she was so supportive that she inspired me to keep going. Eve Eaton suffered through many dry drafts and gently encouraged me to create something more personal. Eve's insights and friendship were a tremendous help throughout the years writing the book, and I continue to treasure them. Richard Martin, whom I had only spoken to once via Skype, generously offered hundreds of detailed comments and made me a better writer in the process. When he said, "This book will help a lot of people," I was inspired to work even harder.

I owe a debt to all the people who worked with me on the individual coaching program and Working Out Loud circles. Patrick Arnold and Barbara Schmidt were the first people I coached, and I'll always remember their patience and encouragement. Mara Tolja formed the first London circle with Anita Sekaran, David Griffin, and Anne-Marie Imafidon, and they shaped the very idea of what a circle could be. My Barcelona circle of Luciano Scorza, Carles Rodrigues, and Meritxell Martinez graciously helped me understand what worked and didn't work. My circle in New York City—Sharon Jurkovich, Nicola Harrison Ruiz, and Melody Browne—helped me practice what I was preaching and turn it into a habit.

Others played a key role in spreading Working Out Loud circles. Christine Burns, Maggie Renz, Jackie Lynton, Helen Sanderson, Carol Read, Michelle Ockers, and Ganesh Ramakrishnan (RG) all took a leap of faith when, based solely on draft materials, they promoted circles to other people. That was important for learning how circles would function, and I'll always be grateful for that. Simon Terry not only promoted circles, he promoted an entire week dedicated to working out loud along with Jonathan Anthony and Austen Hunter. International #wolweek happens every November.

All the people I mentioned in the book inspired me with their stories. I'm honored to have worked with and learned firsthand from Barbara Schmidt, Mara Tolja, Anne-Marie Imafidon, David Griffin, Joyce Sullivan, Nikolay Savvinov, Paul Hewitt, and Hayley Webb. I learned too from those who served as more public examples, including Jordi Muñoz, Brandon Stanton, Fred Wilson, Amanda Palmer, Sandi Ball, and Alycia Zimmerman.

In the notes, I cited a number of researchers and authors who shaped my thinking. Two in particular changed my life: Keith Ferrazzi and Seth Godin. In particular, Keith's course came at a crucial time in my life and helped me see there was a better way to build relationships and discover opportunities. Seth's blog provided me with daily encouragement, so much so that I went up to him after one of his talks to thank him in person and ask for his autograph on a Seth Godin action figure. Embarrassing, perhaps, but true. He signed it "Go make a ruckus."

I'm indebted to Thomas Lukoma, who volunteered to create workingoutloud.com and whose firm, More Than A Hut, helps "regular people do extraordinary things." Together with Melody Browne, he continues to develop new ways to help me reach and engage more people. Danke schön to Jochen Adler for creating workingoutloud.de and helping to spread the word in Germany.

Thank you to Bryce Williams for first writing about "working out loud" in 2010 and generously supporting me and others who use the phrase and spread the idea.

Many people went to the trouble of providing written feedback on my unfinished, unpolished work. That's an extraordinarily generous thing to do. Thank you, Kavi Arasu, Cornelia Bencheton, Helen Blunden, Jonathan Brown, Brigit Calame, Jacqui Chan, Bonnie Cheuk, Marie-Louise Collard, Dany Degrave, Cecil Dijoux, Brandon Ellis, Kathryn Everest, Mark Gadsby, Ravi Ganesh, Maddie Grant, Jessica Hale, John Harwell, Clay Hebert, Ken Hittel, Abigail Hunt, Christopher Isak, Harold Jarche, Irene Johansen, Lois Kelly, Guy Lipman, Anna-Clare Lukoma, Jackie Lynton, Victor Mahler, Jane McConnell, Stuart McIntyre, Ben McMann, Soon Min, Yavor Nikolov, Virpi Oinonen, Thomas Olsen, Vera Olsen, Martin Prusinowski, Päivi Räty, Carol Read, Greg Reilly, Perry Riggs, Kasper Risbjerg, David Robertson, John Rusnak, Samantha Scobie, Susan Scrupski, Ana Silva, Xavier Singy, Suellen Steward, Joachim Stroh, Lisette Sutherland, Kevin Sweeney, David Thompson, and Andrej Vogler. I owe a special debt to Eric Best, a former journalist and author of *Into My Father's Wake*, whose encouragement and editing of my early blog posts inspired me to become a better writer. There are many more people who contributed ideas, feedback, and support, and who read, share, and comment on my weekly posts. I extend my heartfelt thanks to all of them.

Thank you to Kazumi Koyama and Jon Ralphs, who independently applied their creative talents to working out loud and provided the first visual aids I ever used to describe my ideas.

While most authors acknowledge their family's patience and support, my wife, Saori, played a particularly important role in shaping the book. Now she wants to see me spread the benefits of working out loud to education and to the people who need it most.

Finally, there are five important people I am pleased to acknowledge: my children Emily, Adrian, Olivia, Hanako, and Hudson. Every day, they provide me with meaning and fulfillment while also liberally pointing out opportunities for my improvement. Hanako, who celebrated her sixth and seventh birthdays while I was writing, often asked me, "Are you *still* working on *Working Out Loud*?" I will be particularly happy to give her a copy.

About the Author

Author photo: Sartaj Gill

My job is to make work more effective and fulfilling inside a large global bank. That's where I introduced a social collaboration platform and, by applying some of the ideas in this book, helped form a social network used regularly by more than 60,000 people.

The first thing I ever wrote about making work better was *Successful Reengineering*, a book about a holistic approach we used at AT&T Bell Labs. Now I write weekly about management and personal development at johnstepper.com and workingoutloud.com.

Made in the USA
Lexington, KY
18 September 2018